## What people are saying about this book:

"I had never invested in real estate before and all o[f]
and family told me that it was too risky and I shou[ld]
looking at the system and speaking with John pe[r]
I could do it; I knew that I had to do it! Making an
investment property using the WealthLoop syste[m]
the best thing that I ever did. Don't hesitate. If you're serious a[t]
building a financial future, buy the book and do exactly what it tells
you to do!"

"The WealthLoop™ system outlines a method by which
you can create your own personal wealth-building plan,
even if you have very little money to start, and even if
you have no experience whatsoever. It is that simple!"

"I'm on page 32 and hanging on your every word. My husband and
I 'invested' our retirement funds in the market and I have always felt
like it was just a few steps above the slot machines, so I'm with you
on that. I can't wait to see what you have to say next. I AM REALLY
ENJOYING THE BOOK!"

"*Thanks Mr. Michailidis for writing a book that makes sense! I've
found that my own investor clients have been very receptive to your
ideas and I look forward to implementing them into my own real
estate business.*"

"You're very crisp in your presentations and good at
simplifying. There's so much good information that I
went back and read some parts *twice!* It's a great book."

"*Buy this book, read it, implement its techniques, and watch your
financial life change forever!*"

## What people are saying about this book:

"**Wealth is much easier to attain than you think, but you have to plan for it and go after it—this book will show you how!**"

"The key aspects of creating predictable wealth are having a plan, and having proven systems to implement that plan. This book gives you the plan and the systems to begin creating wealth immediately. If you are ready to change your financial life forever, buy this book. But more importantly—use it!"

"*For those wanting to increase their personal wealth while not becoming a slave to their investments, this is the book to read.*"

"**John has written a fine book that cuts through the hype and gets to the meat of what it takes to succeed as a beginning real estate investor.**"

"Being a real estate agent and investor for almost 10 years, I can tell you that the things you will learn in this book will no doubt help you to succeed. Even an 'old dog' like me picked-up a few new ideas."

"*Without a doubt, if you employ the techniques explained in this book you will work less and earn more.*"

"**As a real estate agent I've always preferred working with homebuyers to investors—until I heard about your WealthLoop system. You've come up with a system that is so easy to implement, and that gets investors so excited, that I now find working with investors to be great fun!**"

*The* **WealthLoop**™ *Series*

# Beginner's Guide to
# BUILDING
# WEALTH
## Buying Houses

*The* Foolproof Roadmap
*to* Real Estate Riches
Without *the* Risks
and Hassles *of*
Landlording

## John A. Michailidis, Esq.

Beginner's Guide to Building Wealth Buying Houses
©2007 John A. Michailidis, Esq.

Brain Forge Press™
2106 N. Clark
Chicago, IL  60614

Cover design: George Foster, www.fostercovers.com
Interior design: Liz Tufte, www.folio-bookworks.com

Library of Congress Control Number:  2006907354

ISBN: 0-9788190-9-8
ISBN-13: 978-0-9788190-9-5

Printed in the U.S.A.

This book is dedicated to the workingmen and women who aspire to a life of financial freedom through real estate investing, and to the professional real estate agents who serve them.

# Contents

# Acknowledgements

I was lucky enough to have access to many good people who were willing and eager to help me as I labored at putting this book together. My appreciation goes out to Jay Papasan, co-author with Gary Keller and Dave Jenks of the *Millionaire Real Estate Agent* and *Millionaire Real Estate Investor* books. Jay was kind enough to take the time to share his considerable knowledge of the book industry and to offer a few key suggestions with respect to the project. Based on Jay's advice, the original title was changed to the one we have today.

My appreciation goes out to two good friends, both attorneys, who took the time to review some of these chapters and make many valuable suggestions that found their way into the book. Lee Iglody is one of the best trial attorneys in Las Vegas, Nevada, specializing in business and commercial law. If you need a good trial attorney look him up. Arthur Murphy does general trial work and real estate law in Chicago. If you need a good lawyer in the Chicago area, call Art Murphy.

The administrative staff at Keller Williams Lincoln Park Realty in Chicago acted as my regular sounding board with respect to cover designs, titles, color schemes, etc. Many thanks to Mimi Pfest and Maria Coscia for all of their valuable input. Sue Swift, the office's managing broker, was, as usual, full of enthusiastic support for the project and she also offered valuable suggestions that were incorporated into the book.

My thanks goes out to Kellie Ramsay, Executive Assistant to Mo Anderson, Vice-Chairman of Keller Williams

Realty International. Kellie was just plain nice and helpful, which left an impression on me. Kellie's attitude embodies the win-win spirit that Keller Williams Realty brings to the real estate industry—thanks Kellie!

I was also fortunate to have had much good professional advice. Dan Poynter and John Kremer both offered their expertise. George Foster of Foster Covers in Fairfield, Iowa, designed, in my opinion, the best real estate book cover ever made—thanks George.

Not to be forgotten, I want to thank Phil Tadros and the staff at Dollop coffee shop in Chicago for the innumerable cups of great coffee and free wireless Internet access, without which my task of writing would have been much less enjoyable.

I also wish to thank the many real estate brokers, agents, clients, and customers that I have dealt with during my many years in the real estate industry. I believe that I learned something from each and every one of them.

Finally, I want to thank you, the aspiring real estate investor, for taking the leap of faith to buy this book.

# Disclaimer – Words to the Wise

This book is designed to provide information on certain aspects of real estate investing. It is sold with the understanding that the publisher and author are not engaged in rendering legal, accounting, or other professional services. When legal or other expert assistance is required, you should consult with a competent professional to address your particular situation.

It is not the purpose of this book to reprint all the information that is otherwise available to real estate investors. You are urged to read all the available material, learn as much as possible about real estate investing, and tailor the information to your individual needs.

Real estate investing is not a get-rich-quick scheme. Anyone who decides to invest in real estate must expect to invest a reasonable amount of time and effort.

Every effort has been made to make this book as complete and accurate as possible given the targeted scope of its subject matter. However, this text should only be used as a general guide and not as the ultimate source of real estate investing information. Furthermore, as legal rules and regulations with respect to real estate investing change from time to time, it is the reader's responsibility to ensure that the information contained herein is current as of the time of their reading.

The purpose of this book is to educate and entertain. The author and Brain Forge Press shall have neither liability nor responsibility to any person or entity with respect to loss or damage caused, or alleged to have been caused, directly or indirectly, by the information contained in this book.

# Introduction

## Why I Wrote This Book

As I sit here writing this introduction to my book *Beginner's Guide to Building Wealth Buying Houses*, I feel a little bit self-conscious. The sole purpose of writing this book is to help *you*, the aspiring real estate investor, but by necessity, this introduction must be about me. After all, if you are going to read my book and take me seriously you probably should know a little bit about who I am and why I wrote it. That said, I hope you will bear with me for this brief moment as I talk about myself. Then we can get on to the more important business of getting you started on your journey of creating personal wealth!

Currently I am a licensed Attorney, licensed Real Estate Broker, and licensed Real Estate Licensing Instructor, all in the state of Illinois. Previously I have been licensed as a Real Estate Broker and Real Estate Licensing Instructor in the state of Florida. I earned my first real estate license in 1990 from the state of Nevada. I guess you could say I get around.

I have taught real estate licensing courses for numerous private real estate schools and have taught real estate investing at the college level. I have both owned my own real estate brokerage company and have been the managing broker of a company that I did not own. I was even once the Managing Director of a private real estate school. Over time, I have taught, coached, and mentored numerous aspiring real estate professionals and investors.

While in law school, I took as many real estate related classes as I could, including Property, Real Estate Transactions, Advanced Real Estate Transactions, Real Estate Finance, Zoning and Land Use, and Real Estate Investments. I also hold the GRI designation (Graduate Realtor Institute) and the CRS designation (Certified Residential Specialist), and I am a candidate to receive the CCIM designation (Certified Commercial Investment Member).

Currently I work as a real estate broker in Chicago. My personal niche is representing buyers and sellers of small buildings. A typical transaction that I might be involved in is a six- or seven-unit building with perhaps a few stores on the street level and apartments above . . . you get the idea. A typical price range might be from just under to just over a million dollars, which leads directly into the reason I decided to write this book.

The properties I typically deal in are bought by experienced investors who know what they are doing and have access to capital (money). But "therein lies the rub." Because I have a fairly successful business that is relatively well known in its small niche, and because I spend several thousand dollars a month on marketing and advertising, I get lots of phone calls from people wanting to invest in real estate.

Unfortunately, many of the people who call are not financially able to buy properties at a half-million dollars and above. I'm talking about people who have between $5,000 and $15,000 to invest, have decent credit, and who are extremely motivated to get started. Even though these people have money and credit, I had to turn them away because in our market you just can't find suitable properties for this type of small beginning investor. You have to realize that Chicago prices are high, and in some areas even a tiny studio condominium can sell for over $200,000!

It became important to me to figure out a way to help these smaller, beginning investors. After all, I am in the real estate business and it was killing me to have to turn away all of these ready, willing and able buyers! I had to come up with a plan to help them, and thus I began the process that led to this book.

What I have not yet told you is that for the majority of my early career I sold single-family houses, so I have lots of experience doing that. In fact, in my first full year in real estate I was somewhat of a beginning whiz kid after having sold 33 houses in a town that I had just moved to. (In case you didn't know it, National Association of Realtors® statistics indicate that the average agent sells something like SEVEN properties a year. Unfortunately, most agents either live on the brink of poverty or have another source of income). So, in looking for a way to help beginning investors I began to look back to my experience selling houses.

I knew that the beginning investors who were calling me could not buy into a decent multi-unit investment building in Chicago. I also knew that for various reasons the condominium units available to them were not suitable investments either. Also, if a studio condo can sell for nearly a quarter of a million dollars, you can imagine how much single-family houses in the city can sell for, so these were pretty much out of the question too.

I began looking into smaller communities outside of

Chicago where one could still find a nice little three-bedroom, one-and-a-half bath starter home, with a yard and a basement, for between $100,000 and $150,000—nothing extravagant, just nice. I knew that a small investor could never go wrong investing in the American Dream.

Looking back on my experiences in dealing with hundreds of real estate investors over the years, as well as the extensive real world research I conducted in putting this book together, the *WealthLoop* system was born. I do not know if it is correct to say that I invented the system, in the sense that everything herein is brand new to the world. On the contrary, everything in the system has been tested and proven to work by hundreds and possibly thousands of successful real estate investors. Right now there are untold numbers of people building personal wealth with the techniques you are about to learn!

I think it is more accurate to say that I brought all of the pieces together into one integrated system that takes the guesswork out of investing and gives you a specific, tested, and proven roadmap to follow on your path to personal wealth creation. There is no need for you to reinvent the wheel. Just follow the plan and you will create wealth.

Part I of this book is not particularly about the *Wealth-Loop* system but covers the basics of investing, investments, and real estate. My intention is to first help you see the investing world as I do, and only then do I move on to specifics. I spend a good bit of time going over definitions and discussing the particular point of view that I feel will enable you to maximize your use of the specific techniques presented in Part II. It is my opinion that this basic foundation will best equip you to truly understand the nature and power of the *WealthLoop* approach to real estate investing.

Finally, I want to let you know right up front that my writing style is unconventional. I expect you to get involved and to participate in a dialogue with me, as much as this is possible to do while reading a book.

I am going to challenge many of the things you were told about investing and some of the things I say might ruffle your feathers a bit. To that I say, "Good!" I want you to THINK. I want you to LEARN. I want you to QUESTION conventional wisdom. And in the end, I want you to become FINANCIALLY FREE. For that, I am willing to risk ruffling your feathers.

So sit back, concentrate, and get ready to learn and master a proven wealth-building system that is sure to change your life.

## Welcome to the *WealthLoop* . . .

# Part I

# Chapter 1

## Just in Case You Didn't Already Know, The Economic Game is Rigged Against You!

The game is rigged! The day I fully and completely understood the truth of this statement marked a personal turning point in my outlook towards work, jobs, investing, and how wealth is actually created. I realized that nearly everything I heard on the financial news channels and read in the financial press was lies, half-truths, and more lies. I realized that the mainstream education and training that we all receive in our modern western society is completely and undeniably geared towards creating good little workers and savers, not millionaires.

True wealth creation is rarely, if ever, mentioned in the mainstream press, or in school, and then always in a way that makes it sound as though it's reserved for superhuman businessmen like Bill Gates or Warren Buffet, or mega-star entertainers like Barbara Streisand or Brad Pitt. Stories about normal men and women just like you and me who are creating wealth are hard to find. I know for a fact that such people exist. I know that there are multitudes of normal folks who have broken free from the rat race and managed to create true wealth for themselves and their families, but it is clear that the social "powers that be" want to keep these stories under wraps. Let's take a deeper look.

Did you learn about creating personal wealth for yourself in high school? How about in college? When was the last time you heard a news story about a "little guy" who managed to break away from the crowd and create a meaningful independent income for himself? Why do you think such stories aren't publicized? Why do you think creating wealth isn't taught in schools?

Perhaps one reason why public schools don't teach this is that it's just too hard. Harder than physics? Harder than calculus, or algebra? That's nonsense, complete nonsense! The principles of wealth creation are simple and straightforward—much simpler and easier than calculating the rate of change of an accelerating celestial body (calculus), or trying to figure out which train gets to Cincinnati first (algebra)!

Take me as an example. I was never taught a thing about personal wealth creation in high school. I went on to college, where I majored in economics and business for heaven's sake, and still was never taught anything about personal wealth creation. Finally, I went to Northwestern University School of Law, where they taught me about property, contracts, taxation, mergers and acquisitions, but nothing specifically about personal wealth creation. I've been a reader of the Wall Street Journal, Fortune, Forbes, the Financial Times, etc., but can't say that I've read much about personal wealth creation in those publications.

Now, I have to admit that in all of my schooling and reading I have learned things that are helpful with respect to creating personal wealth. I am most certainly not saying that nothing I learned or read was relevant, but I can tell you without a doubt that never once was I taught how to put it all together, to create a system and a plan for creating personal wealth. That was something I had to do for myself, through much trial and error. I created the *Wealth-Loop* system so that you do not have to go through all the pain and aggravation that I did.

Have you considered the possibility that the reason they do not teach us about wealth creation in school is that they do not want us to know how to do it? Do you think that the reason the financial press covers big business, corporations, and the stock market instead of personal wealth creation is that they want to brainwash us into being beholden to the corporations for our livelihood, and they want us to funnel our meager wages back into the corporations by putting what little we have left over into corporate stocks, bonds, IRA's, and 401k's?

Think about it from the corporation's view. They make us depend on them for our income. Then they do their damnedest to take back that income through their relentless marketing that trains us to be unhappy unless we buy the latest new gadgets they are selling. They use the financial press to persuade us to by stocks, stocks, and more stocks.

It's a great racket for the corporations, it's the greatest racket ever created! Oh, and let's take it a step further: let's not forget the banks and credit card companies that do their best to keep us in debt up to our eyeballs so that we never have a chance of breaking free and creating true personal wealth. I'll say it again: The Economic Game is Rigged Against You!

But there is a way out. It may not be publicized, but many ordinary men and women have found their way to financial freedom. However, before we get into the nitty-gritty details of how to create personal wealth for you and your family, let's create a working definition of what we're after . . .

# Chapter 2

## Tilting the Odds in Your Favor –
## Creating a WealthLoop™

What is wealth anyway? On the face of it, it appears to be a simple enough question, but is it really? Is it a particular amount of money in the bank? Is it a certain salary level? Is wealth a lifestyle? An attitude? Is it happiness? Is it health? Is it time freedom? So that you and I are on the same "sheet of music" with respect to the meaning of wealth, let's agree on a working definition. What do you think of this:

> "Wealth means having automatic income streams that are independent of your personal labor, and that are sufficient to maintain your chosen individual lifestyle indefinitely."

This is what I call a *WealthLoop*.

Let's break it down. The first aspect of a *WealthLoop* are *automatic income streams*. The concept of automatic income streams is easy enough to understand. It means that a predictable amount of money comes to you on a continuous and regular basis, without interruption, without fluctuation, and from more than one source.

If you have automatic income you know exactly how much money you will be getting and when you will be getting it. You don't have to think about it; it just comes! If you have such automatic income from multiple sources that are not dependent on each other, then you don't have to worry too much about your financial security. Multiple income streams keep you from putting all of your eggs in one basket, which helps you minimize your risk.

The next key component of our working definition of wealth is that the automatic income streams have to be *independent of your personal labor*. After all, if you have all the money in the world coming in, but in order to get it you have to work 20 hours a day at four different jobs, would you really consider yourself wealthy?

This is a very important point with respect to wealth. It is important because most of us equate wealth with *freedom*, which has become a modern cliché but one well worth mentioning here. Haven't we all heard of the wealthy executive who is tied to his job 80 hours a week, rarely sees his kids, has no relationship to speak of with his wife, drinks too much, is out of shape, and is generally unhappy with life?

I think you will agree that automatic income, in and of itself, does not constitute wealth. We need to add the condition that your automatic income be *independent of your personal labor*. Once that happens you are starting to get somewhere! At that point you will have income coming in whether you sleep all day, go fishing, play with your kids, make love, or watch TV.

Would you agree that an important aspect of wealth is having the freedom to do what you want to do, whenever you want to do it? Surely you can see that there is more to creating wealth than simply creating automatic income streams. Wealth is also about having the *time* to enjoy your income, which is why a condition for creating a *WealthLoop* is that your automatic income streams be independent of your personal labor.

Being independent of your personal labor does not mean that you will never have to do anything with respect to your income streams, but that you will not have to punch a clock or organize your life according to somebody else's plans and schedules. You will be in charge of what you do and when you do it. Other people will conform to your schedules rather than you conforming to theirs.

With that said, are independent income streams alone enough to constitute wealth? What if you did have regular checks coming in from various sources, every single month that were generated completely independently of your own personal labor? Could you finally say that you were wealthy? Well, maybe yes; but maybe no. You would still need to address the *amount* of income necessary for you to maintain *your* chosen lifestyle. Multiple streams of independent income are always good to have, but if they are not enough to cover your bills you cannot consider yourself wealthy.

If you have built a true *WealthLoop* you must have developed independent income streams that are *sufficient to maintain your chosen individual lifestyle indefinitely.* Common sense tells you that just because you have regular checks coming in, even if they are completely independent of your personal labor, if those checks are only for $1.47

each you are not wealthy. Wealth is also about *maintaining your chosen lifestyle indefinitely.*

Some people get bogged down on this point by trying to come up with a particular number that is "the amount of money" required to be considered wealthy. Well, there is no particular amount, or more accurately, there are as many particular amounts as there are people. Once your income is regular, independent, and comes from multiple sources, you can decide on the amount that constitutes wealth for YOU.

Do you want to have mansions, jet planes and helicopters? If so, the amount of income you need to be wealthy will be very high. But if you are like most people, then all you really want is a nice home with all of the creature comforts, a few nice "toys" in the garage, time to take vacations and indulge your interests and hobbies, and the security of knowing that no matter what happens you will have the financial resources to take care of your family. Wealth is much easier to attain than you think, but you have to plan for it and go after it. It is not going to just happen on its own.

I suggest that a good goal to strive for is simply replacing all of the income currently generated by your job with income that is independently and automatically generated from multiple sources. If you do that, your life will be yours to do with, as you like!

You can quit your job if you want. You can set your sights on finding ways to generate higher and higher amounts of income if that is what excites you. Or, you can just sit back and live the same life you have always lived; only now you can live it completely free from the stress of financial worries and time pressures. The choice is yours.

As you can see, creating wealth is about predictability,

regularity, and independence. It is about having a plan in place, and using whatever systems may be necessary so that you will know exactly when and how much income will be coming in. The systems (which you will be learning throughout the book) are important, because they are what will allow you to place your income generation plan on autopilot, thus freeing you from having to "work" for a living.

While it might never be possible to have 100% certainty with respect to anything in life, the key aspects of creating predictable wealth include having a plan, having systems to implement your plan, and then working your plan. This book takes care of the first two for you, but it is up to you to work the plan.

The *WealthLoop*™ system will teach you how to create:

- Automatic income streams,
- which are largely independent of your personal labor,
- that can be scaled to support your chosen individual lifestyle indefinitely.

You will learn how to break free from the rat race, gain control of your income and your time, and live the lifestyle you were meant to live. Let us begin . . .

# Chapter 3

## How Does One Create Personal Wealth?

N ow that we have defined wealth, the next logical question is how does one go about creating it? It is one thing to say that you have to create independent income streams, and quite another thing to put that advice into practice. So, how might *you* go about creating *automatic income streams* that are *independent of your personal labor* and that are *sufficient to maintain your chosen individual lifestyle indefinitely?*

The financial press and so-called financial gurus and pundits talk about investing, which to them typically involves corporate stocks and related items such as mutual funds and 401k's. So that you are not misled by all of the hype and misinformation that is out there, we are going to discuss some key terms and then relate them to how effective they might be in your quest to create sustainable personal wealth for you.

When you think about it, there are only so many ways you can accumulate money. You could steal it. You could find it. Somebody could just give it to you as a gift or inheritance. You could invent something that other people want and sell it to them, such as a machine. Or it could be a song or a book or a piece of computer software—we call this intellectual property. You could trade your labor for money—that's what we call a job. You could gamble with money you already have in the hopes of winning back even more money—that's what we call speculation. You could put money that you already have to work for you in generating income, thus creating even more money—that's what we call investing.

So that's it. The only ways to accumulate money are to steal it, find it, receive it as a gift, create intellectual property, work for it, speculate, or invest. I want you to really think about this. I want you to truly understand that there are ONLY SEVEN POSSIBLE WAYS TO ACCUMULATE MONEY!

I'll bet you thought there were infinite ways, but that's not true at all. While there might be infinite ways to invest or speculate or invent or steal, ultimately, no matter what you do, it must fit into one of these seven basic categories. This fact makes it very easy for us to narrow down the possibilities and to find the most efficient way for you to begin the process of accumulating personal wealth.

Now that you know that there are only seven possible ways to accumulate money, we can begin to look into each of these ways to see which might be the best ways for you to create sustainable wealth for yourself. First, let's consider theft. Isn't theft one way of accumulating money and income? Sure it is, but is it a valid method of wealth creation? Well, for some people, and all governments, it is a way of accumulating wealth. However, an honest person will accept the fact that for any method of wealth creation to be considered legitimate it cannot involve force, fraud, threats, or lies.

All of our transactions must be voluntary and "win-win" between all parties involved. Unlike governments and thieves, we cannot demand of others that they hand over their money, and we certainly cannot unilaterally take money by threatening violence or imprisonment. As far as you and I are concerned, let's scratch theft off the list of viable routes to personal wealth creation.

So, what about finding a big pile of money? It certainly is possible, but do you want to stake your financial future on it? Is the likelihood of finding money *predictable* and *regular*? If not, we have to scratch it off of our list of realistic possible paths to personal wealth.

What about receiving a big inheritance or gift? Well, the chances are that if you are in line for a big inheritance you already know about it. Truth be told, if a huge fortune awaits you then you probably don't need this book! Unfortunately, for the vast majority of people, receiving a large gift or inheritance just isn't going to happen. So we have to scratch it off our list of sustainable paths to personal wealth.

Have you noticed that three of the seven possible ways of creating wealth are not practical at all? Having narrowed the field of possible paths to wealth down to just four, let's take a look at these four remaining possibilities: intellectual property, personal labor, speculation, and investing.

The first of these, intellectual property (inventing something) is one possible path to wealth. In fact, intellectual property is one of the best paths to wealth creation. If you write a bestselling novel (or real estate investing book), each time a copy sells you would get paid! The same applies if you record a hit song. Every time a copy of the song gets sold or is played on the radio, you would get paid!

What if you invented a new machine or technology? You would have the right to patent your invention, which would allow you to lock-up the reproduction rights. You could either market your invention yourself or you could rent your rights to others who would market your invention and pay you a royalty on all of their sales (this is called licensing).

Whether it's songs, books, technologies, movies, software, etc., the thing that makes intellectual property such a powerful wealth creator is that you only have to produce your idea ONCE. However, you get to sell it OVER AND OVER AND OVER AGAIN!

Think of a movie star. An actor only has to make a movie once, yet he or she will get paid every time it is shown in a theatre, rented at the video store, or played on TV. By now you realize that repeatability is a key requirement of wealth creation.

In addition to the repeatability of generating income through the creation of intellectual property, can you see how completely different income streams might also be generated from the same intellectual property? Let's go back to the movie example, where it happens all the time. Not only do the movie studios make money from the film itself, but also from merchandise such as Tee shirts, action-figures, posters, movie soundtracks, sequels, and so on.

Now, back to reality. Not everyone is going to make a movie, write a book, or build a better mousetrap. Maybe you have it in you and maybe you don't. Unless you are a creative person with time on your hands, you are probably not going to make your fortune by creating intellectual property. However, as you embark on your personal wealth creation journey it is important that you understand your options—all of your options—so that you can follow the path that's right for you. Who really knows what the future will bring?

Even if intellectual property creation isn't your path to wealth, keep it in the back of your mind. I want you to remember what makes it so powerful—it's repeatable, it can be duplicated, and it can be used to generate income from various sources. Once we get through our basic overview of wealth creation I'll show you how to create your own wealth-building plan using these same principles as laid out in the *WealthLoop* system.

Let's do a quick recap. So far we've discovered that theft isn't a viable way for you to create personal wealth. Neither is hoping to find a big pile of cash. We know that the likelihood of your inheriting a large sum of money is slim to none, and unless you are very creative and talented with a lot of time on your hands, you are not going to create wealth through intellectual property creation. We have completely eliminated four of the seven possible paths to wealth, so let's analyze the remaining three: labor, speculation, and investing.

The first one is easy. If there is one thing you probably know like the back of your hand, it's personal labor. If you are like me, you have probably had a job since you were a teenager. Your parents probably told you to study hard and get good grades so you could get a good job.

You may have pursued specialized training in accounting, plumbing, or law – all in the hopes of improving your chances of landing a great job. So, let me ask you, are you wealthy yet? Okay, so let me ask you this, do you foresee EVER becoming wealthy from your job?

I believe I know your answer. If you had even the slightest chance of getting rich from your job you would probably not be reading this book! So, how come, in spite of everything you have ever been told about working hard and getting a good job, is it such a horrible path to take if your intention is to achieve sustainable wealth? Come to think of it, if hardly anybody ever gets rich from their job, why is there so much emphasis in school, from the media, and from society in general to get a job?

We have already touched on the answer to the second question. The reason why schools, the media, and society in general emphasize employment (jobs) over entrepreneurship (creating wealth) is that the powers that be (corporations and the government) make a killing off the labor of employees, but benefit comparatively little from the work of independent wealth creators. In other words, the government and big corporations make lots of money from employees, so the schools and the media (which are respectively: government and corporate entities) continuously push the idea of employment over personal wealth creation.

The entire system is rigged against employees, but favors big corporations and government. The tax system disfavors employees (which is why the government makes such a killing on taxing employees). The corporations generate massive amounts of income at the same time that they are cutting wages, cutting benefits, and sending high paying jobs offshore. While I could write an entire book about how the system is rigged against the working man and woman, suffice it to say that if jobs are so great how come less people than ever before are feeling financially secure?

Another thing about jobs is that they are about trading

time for money, and since there are only so many hours in a day, no matter how good a job you have you are going to eventually max-out your income. Even if you are a brain surgeon making $2,000 an hour, you cannot work 24/7.

Most people do not realize that those professionals that end up actually achieving wealth do so outside of their jobs. They invest the income from their jobs, so that their money is making money for them. *Their jobs are not what make them wealthy; their investments are what make them wealthy.* We'll talk more about investing, but first let's talk about speculation.

In an economic sense, what does it mean to speculate? A useful example to help define speculation is the lottery. Let's face it, we might (if we play) win the Mega-Lotto for three hundred million dollars and be set for life! I think we can agree that this is one way to accumulate a fortune, but how likely is it? This method of wealth creation is called speculation. Speculation means that your return is based on chance, and the problem with chance is that you cannot control it, plan for it, or depend on it.

Speculation is the same as gambling. If I were at a casino and placed a bet on "19/red" at the roulette table, the outcome would be completely out of my hands. I might win, or I might loose, but I certainly would not have any control over the outcome. Furthermore, even if I did win, the likelihood that I would win the next time I bet on 19/red would be quite small. Speculation and gambling are the same thing in that they are not repeatable with certainty; they are governed by the randomness of chance.

Unfortunately, many, many people confuse speculation with investing. The really sad thing is that the financial media regularly perpetrates massive fraud by characterizing speculative activities as investments. They simply lie, and most people believe them.

Here is what I mean; if you take money and put it into the stock of a company that you have no control over, a company that has no obligation to pay you any of their earnings or profits, so that the only hope you have of making your money back is IF the value of your stock goes up and you sell it, is that an investment or a speculation?

Look at this again:

- You have no control over what the company does;
- They have no obligation to pay you your money back;
- The only way you make money is if the stock goes up in value and you are able to sell it.

So, what is the difference between putting your money into the stock of this company and putting it on "19/red" on the roulette table? I tell you that there is absolutely no difference whatsoever, and yet the financial media will swear that this is an investment! Well I am here to tell you that this is a pure speculation, not an investment. It is gambling!

Do not let yourself be fooled by the liars who tell you otherwise. They are looking to steal your money away from you, and to keep you from becoming wealthy. Because the game is rigged, they can get away with it. Sure, sometimes somebody hits it big, just like sometimes somebody hits the "Mega-Lotto," but speculation is no way to ensure your future wealth.

Here's another example. What if you "placed a bet" on Enron stock back in 1999? I'm sure you know that if you had placed such a bet you would have "crapped out" and lost all of your "investment," just like the millions of people who lost everything when the company went bust. The Enron example should make it absolutely clear to you that buying stocks on the stock market is a pure gamble. If you want to gamble that is fine, but do not fool yourself into thinking that you are investing when you are not.

Before we move on to an explanation of investing, I want to clarify something about stocks. You might wonder why stocks are touted as a good investment. The answer is that they are an excellent investment for those who CREATE and SELL STOCKS to people like you! Those are the only people who are virtually guaranteed to make money on stocks—everybody else is gambling.

Think about it from the big corporation's point of view. You get to create pieces of paper that you sell to people for money. You have no obligation to pay those people back, and you can do whatever you want to do with the money. It is the biggest con game on earth! Actually, it's the second biggest—the printing of paper money by governments is the biggest con game on earth, but that story is beyond the scope of this book.

Now do you see why the financial media, corporations, and the powers that be push stocks? It is because they want to steal your money!

So, let's review. We have ruled out theft, finding money, and getting a huge inheritance as likely paths for you to build sustainable personal wealth. Common sense and personal experience prove to you that speculation and jobs might be ways to get money, but these are certainly not guaranteed paths to wealth. We have shown that intellectual property is an excellent path to wealth creation, but we have also noted that the creation of intellectual property takes time and talent that most people just do not have.

At this point, we have ruled out SIX of the seven possible paths for creating sustainable personal wealth. By now I hope that you realize that if you want to change your financial future you are going to have to start focusing your energies on the one path that offers you a legitimate shot—investing. Investing is the only proven path to sustainable wealth creation that *anyone* can undertake regardless of his or her level of formal education, amount of money in the bank, or talent. The truth is that investing is actually *easy* once you understand what it is and what it is not. The *WealthLoop* system outlines a method by which you can create your own personal wealth-building plan, even if you have very little money to start, and even if you have no experience whatsoever. It is that simple!

So, what is *investing*? What does it mean to *invest*, or to be an *investor*? I'm not talking about the fraudulent definition we hear from public educators and the media, but the true definition. Let's take a look.

I want you to imagine something. Imagine a machine that creates money. In one end of this magical machine you put some raw materials that are worth relatively few dollars and out the other end pops a big pile of cash! Like any machine, you have to make sure that you keep it clean and well oiled, change the belts occasionally, and do other routine maintenance tasks, but as long as you are attentive to its upkeep and you keep feeding raw materials into one end of the machine, money always pops out of the other end! It's a money machine!

This mythical money machine is what we call an *asset*. *An asset is anything that generates more income than it costs to control.* If you have something that costs you $100 per month to own and maintain, but it generates $300 per month of income, then you have an asset. The excess of income over the cost of ownership is called *positive income* or *net income*. In the above example, you control something that generates $300 per month, but it only costs you $100 per month. In this case, the difference between the amount you make and the amount it costs you is $200, which is your *net income* from this asset.

An asset can be anything. If you own a bulldozer that costs you $2,000 per month to own and maintain, but you are able to rent that bulldozer out to contractors for $800 per week ($800 x 4 = $3,200), then your bulldozer is an asset. If you own a piece of land that costs you $1,000 per month to own and maintain, but you are able to rent it out as 20 parking spaces for $75 per month each (20 x $75 = $1,500) then you have an asset.

Whenever you are able to control an asset (through buying it, or maybe even just renting it -- it really doesn't matter how you are able to control the asset, so long as the cost of controlling it is less than the income it generates for you) then you are *investing*. An investment is money that you spend to control an asset. An asset is something that generates more income that it costs. An asset is a *money machine.*

Understand that any particular thing can be either an asset, or not, depending on whether or not it generates income. Take a house for example. If you are personally living in the house, then it is NOT an asset! Don't be confused by this, just ask yourself this question: "If I live in the house, is it generating income"?

Since the house is obviously not generating income if you are living in it, it does not meet the definition of an asset. However, if you take the exact same house and rent it out for more money then it costs you to own, then it is an asset. Think about it.

Truth be told, many people get agitated when I tell them that their house is not an asset. They tell me things like, "It's gone up over $50,000 in value since I bought it, and it's the most valuable thing I own!" To this I answer, "Great!" But assets generate income. End of story. Yes your house is valuable, and yes I recommend that EVERYBODY own his or her own house—just don't call it an asset or consider it an investment when it's not. [Hint: Rich people understand the difference — that's why they're rich!]

Notice that an investment is VERY DIFFERENT THAN A SPECULATION! If you buy 10 ounces of gold in the hopes that you will make money on the deal, is that an investment, or a speculation? Well here is the test. Take your 10 ounces of gold to the bank, put them in a safety deposit box and come back in a month. Open the safety deposit box in a month and see if more than 10 ounces of gold are now inside. If there are still only 10 ounces, then it is not an investment!

No income generation means that it is not an investment. I do not care if you leave it sitting in the safety deposit box for 100 years, unless you can open up that box in 100 years and find more than 10 ounces of gold inside, then it is not an investment.

Perhaps at the end of 100 years the value of the gold went up. If it does you will have made money, but realize that you made money on a *speculation*, not an investment. Investing means that you are actually generating income from an asset; it does not mean that you might make money if you get lucky and the thing you own goes up in value. After all, is hoping that the value of gold goes up not the same as hoping that you hit "19/red" at the roulette table? Is it not just a gamble?

By now it should be clear to you that the best and most practical path to personal wealth creation is through investing. I hope that I have successfully drummed it into you that an investment must actually generate income, and it must generate more income than it costs to control, which brings us to one final point about assets.

What makes any asset a good investment? Let's look at the economic forces that allow any asset to generate income.

You know that an asset must generate positive income to be a good investment, but have you thought about the economic characteristics of an asset that allow it to generate income? What economic characteristics cause one thing to be able to generate income, but keep another thing from generating income?

The ability of an asset to generate income is based on two economic market forces: supply and demand. By supply we simply mean the availability of an asset on the open market; are there a lot of these assets available to the market, or is the asset hard to find? By demand we simply mean the desire of people in the market to have (buy, rent, or use) the asset; do a lot of people want the asset, or could people care less if the asset is available?

The two market forces of supply and demand work together to determine an asset's market value. And because income generation is directly related to value, these forces also determine an asset's ability to generate income. (Assets of little value can only generate little income, and assets of great value can generate great amounts of income.)

If an asset is really in demand (I mean EVERYBODY wants it badly) do you think that would tend to increase, or decrease the asset's value? If an asset had very little demand (I mean NOBODY wants it) how do you think that would affect its value?

If you were in the middle of the Sahara Desert, would you be willing to pay more for a glass of water than if you were on a houseboat in the middle of Lake Michigan? I suspect that your demand for water would be much higher in the desert than on the lake, and I bet that you would be willing to pay almost anything for a glass of water in the desert, but close to nothing for a glass of water on the lake.

In this example, your demand for water is vastly different depending on its availability, which means that the value of the water to you is also vastly different depending on its availability. Another word for availability is *supply.*

Notice how the supply of water comes into play here. If you were in the Sahara Desert, but this time you had an inexhaustible supply of water with you, how much would you be willing to pay someone for a glass of water? I suspect that you would not be willing to pay anything for a glass of water in this circumstance. Your demand for water would be very low, because as far as you are concerned, water is abundant (there is an endless supply) and you have more than you could ever need, so why pay for another glass?

Understanding how supply and demand intertwine to affect value, let's look at how it affects income. In this example, you are not the buyer of a glass of water, but the seller. Assume that you control the only fresh water supply in all of the Sahara Desert—if anybody wants a glass of water they have to see you! How much do you think you could charge for a glass of water? I suspect that you could charge a very high price, which means you could generate a lot of income.

Now imagine that you are in the middle of Lake Michigan. How much do you think you could charge for a glass of water? I suspect that you could not even give a glass away, which means that you could not generate any income. Think about it a little bit. Make up some examples of your own, and keep these principles in mind as we begin to discuss real estate investing.

The questions you should now be asking yourself are:
1) Are certain assets easier and safer to invest in than others, and
2) How can I get started?

For all practical purposes, for the average man or woman there are only two realistic types of investments. Think about it. Are you going to buy aircraft and lease them to the airlines? Are you going to buy an oil well and lease the drilling rights to an oil company? Are you going to buy the rights to a movie and collect the royalties? Are you going to buy a company's receivables for forty cents on the dollar and then go out and collect the receivables? Are you going to buy stage lighting and rent it to rock bands on the weekends?

There are a lot of assets that can be purchased, but how practical are these assets for the average person? Realistically speaking, either you are going to invest in a business, or you are going to invest in real estate. That said, let's look at businesses first.

Businesses are assets. Restaurants, shoe stores, insurance agencies, and on and on. A business is nothing more than a system for generating income. The raw materials are people, inventory, management skills, accounting, marketing, distribution networks, customer service, equipment, supplies, legal agreements, etc. Take all of these raw materials and put them into one end of the business money-machine and out of the other end pops profits! Well, maybe.

The problem with getting started on your path to personal wealth creation through businesses is that they are typically expensive to start or buy, require a multitude of different types of skills to operate effectively, and if you don't do everything just right, the odds are extremely high that you will go bust and loose everything. You have probably heard the well-proven statistic that over 80% of new businesses fail within their first few years. Like I said, businesses are tough.

You need inventory, you need a location, and you have all of the legal fees, permits, and licenses to contend with. Start-up costs could easily be many tens, or hundreds of thousands of dollars and that is before you have even found your first customer. What about skills? You need administrators to do the paperwork, salespeople to do the selling, bookkeepers to keep track of everything. How many people do you know who are good at all of these things? In fact, this is a classic mistake of people who start their own business, and a major reason why most businesses fail.

Here is a typical example. A guy is a good mechanic. He thinks that being a good mechanic is the main ingredient for opening a mechanic shop. Wrong! Knowing how to operate a business is the main ingredient for opening a mechanic shop! Anybody can hire a good mechanic, but relatively few people can operate a successful mechanic shop. So, the guy opens his own shop and before you know it he is in over his head. Not only is he dealing with issues that he has no experience dealing with, but because of all his other responsibilities he does not even have the time to do the one thing that he really is good at, which is fixing cars. He is a statistic waiting to happen, just like the thousands and thousands of other businesses that go bust every year.

Worse yet in my opinion, suppose that our mechanic friend does manage to scratch out a living. So, now what does he have? Does he have an investment? The answer is no! He has a job! Remember that the whole point is to become financially free. If you have to go to work everyday you are not an investor, you are a worker. This mechanic traded one job for another, but now, since he "owns" this job, he never feels like he can take a day off. All of the responsibilities fall on his shoulders, and in the end he finds himself worse off than if he would have stayed with his old boss and collected a paycheck.

The truth is that at least 95% of the people that think they are starting a business are actually just starting a new job for themselves. You do not want to do this. You want to have multiple income streams that are independent of your physical labor. Unless you have the money to purchase existing businesses and hire professional managers, businesses are probably not the best way to *begin* as an investor. So, what is an "average Joe or Jane" to do? Let's talk about real estate . . .

# Chapter 4

## What Makes Real Estate Such a Good Investment?

First, let's define the term. What is "real estate"? Can you come up with a comprehensive definition? Like most people, you probably never really thought about it all that much. I suspect that you will be quite surprised by how all encompassing the answer actually is:

> *Real estate includes "land," which is the surface of the earth (including all naturally occurring bodies of water and naturally growing vegetation) everything below the surface of the earth to the earth's center, everything above the earth's surface to infinity, plus anything manmade that is permanently attached to land.*

That is a whole lot! All of the naturally occurring trees and bushes are land. All of the rivers, lakes and oceans are land. All of the air above the surface of the earth is land. All of the rocks in the ground are land. All of the oil in the ground is land.

You may have never thought about the fact that if you

own some land you own the air above it, but if you think about it, it makes sense. That is what allows you to go up and build a skyscraper, and what keeps your neighbor from being allowed to build a balcony over your property line. This is called *air rights*.

You may have never thought about the fact that if you own land you own everything below the surface to the center of the earth, but if you think about it, it makes sense. That is what allows you to drill for and pump oil on your property, or dig for copper, or drill a water well—you own everything under there! This is called *subsurface rights* or *mineral rights*.

If you build something on, under, or above land, then we call the land itself plus whatever you built "real estate." Land by itself only includes naturally occurring things, so the minute you build something and permanently attach it to the land we have to come up with a new definition.

> *"Real estate" is land plus all permanently attached manmade objects.*

Understand that what a particular thing "is" has nothing to do with whether or not it is considered real estate; being "permanently attached to land" is what makes something real estate or not. A door that is lying in the back of your truck is just a door, *but once you attach it to a building the door itself becomes real estate.*

As completely ridiculous as it may sound, if you dig a hole, throw in a can of tuna fish, and then fill the hole with cement such that the can of tuna fish becomes permanently attached to the land, *then the can of tuna fish is now real estate!* (There is an exception to this *attachment rule* in as much as the law recognizes something called a *trade fixture*, but we need not concern ourselves with that here).

Put a building on land and you have real estate (everything permanently attached to the building is also real estate). Build a pipeline under land and you have real estate (everything permanently attached to the pipeline is also real estate). Put plants on land that were not there naturally (farms, orchards, vineyards, etc.) and you have real estate. Put a fence around a field and you have real estate (everything permanently attached to the fence is also real estate).

What a definition! Open your eyes and you are looking at land/real estate! If you are in a room, you are in land/real estate. If you are in a lake, you are in land/real estate. If you are in a cave, you are in land/real estate. Stores, buildings, houses, factories, farms, parks, parking lots, in-ground swimming pools, airports, churches, police stations, mansions, and golf courses are all real estate!

What makes real estate a good investment you ask? Could it be that everywhere you find people, real estate is in great demand? Think back to our previous discussion about how demand affects value. People need places to live, work, shop, grow food, raise livestock, and even take vacations. There is a huge demand for real estate anywhere people want to be, which makes it very, very valuable. If you can control real estate in a place where people want to be, then you have a very good chance of getting rich!

What about supply? At first blush you might be tempted to say that the supply of real estate is unlimited. After all, the entire planet and everything built on it is land/real estate. However, if you look at the way people actually use real estate you will come to the rather paradoxical conclusion that for all practical purposes real estate is a scarce resource.

First of all, not all real estate can be used interchangeably. There are agricultural properties, residential properties, industrial properties, commercial properties, and retail properties. If I am a builder of single-family houses, I am not going to bother looking at office buildings. If I am starting a cattle ranch I am not going to look at single-family houses. The number of properties available for any particular user is limited by the type of property he or she is looking for.

Secondly, there is truth to the old real estate cliché—location, location, location! People do not so much set out to look for a particular piece of real estate as they look for a particular city, town, neighborhood, district, or street. Only after they have narrowed things down to a particular area do they then consider particular properties.

If people did not care about location, all real estate would be considered exactly the same, and you could say that it was abundant. However, the fact that location is typically the user's first consideration means that many properties will be ruled out from the start. This fact sets us up for the reality that any particular user typically finds himself or herself confronted with only a limited number of real estate choices. This flies in the face of our first blush assumption that real estate is abundant.

Combine the facts that real estate choices are based on both property type and location, and it becomes apparent that real estate is in fact scarce as far as any particular user is concerned. Imagine that you are a garment manufacturer that needs to find a manufacturing building in the garment district. Because of your particular requirements there are actually only a limited number of potential properties for you to look at. As far as you are concerned, real estate is scarce.

Add to this the fact that other garment manufacturers are likely to also be in need of the same type of property in the same area, and you can see that the combined forces of supply and demand conspire to make real estate a quite valuable commodity. It is both scarce and in high demand!

So far, you know that for something to be considered a good investment it must generate a positive income. You also know that the ability of an asset to generate positive income is tied to its value – the more valuable an asset, the more income it is likely to generate. Finally, you have seen how the combined forces of supply and demand conspire to make real estate a valuable asset.

Given the fact that real estate meets the first test of a good investment—it is valuable and therefore able to generate income—let's look at other factors that combine to make real estate the very best investment for the average investor.

When an asset is purchased using borrowed money we say that it was purchased using *leverage*. And one thing that makes real estate such an attractive investment is the ability of investors to use leverage to buy properties. It is relatively easy to borrow money to purchase real estate. The average person with average credit (depending on property type) can typically borrow between 75 and 90 percent of the cost of a property. A person with above average credit can often borrow between 95 and 100 percent of the cost of certain types of property.

This ability to easily use leverage to buy real estate is a

huge advantage. You can control valuable real estate for between zero and twenty-five cents on the dollar! If you are not a "financial person" then you might not realize how much of a boost this can give to your return on investment. Imagine a situation where you purchase an asset with $100,000 of your own money. To make the numbers easy, imagine that your *net operating income* (income after all expenses) on the property is $10,000 per year. In this case you made $10,000 on a $100,000 investment, which is to say that you made a 10 percent return on your investment.

Now imagine that you used leverage to purchase the same $100,000 property. Let's say that you put down $10,000 of your own money and borrowed $90,000. Let's say that your payments on the $90,000 are $525 a month, which comes to $6,300 a year. Because you have to make the loan payments, your income of $10,000 has to be reduced by $6,300, so your net operating income is $3,700.

Let's compare both sets of numbers. In the first example where you used only your own money, your net income was $10,000 on an investment of $100,000—your return on investment was 10 percent. In the second example, where you borrowed $90,000 using leverage, your net income was $3,700 on an investment of $10,000—your return was 37 percent. You almost *quadrupled* your return using leverage!

There is another subtle, yet powerful benefit to leverage that you may not have considered. If you are lucky enough to actually have $100,000 to invest and you put it all into the one property in our example, then the most you would make in the year is $10,000. However, if you can control a property for only $10,000 through the use of leverage, why not divide up your $100,000 and put down $10,000 on each of ten properties? According to our above example you would be making $3,700 from each of your ten properties, which means you would be making $37,000 a year instead of only $10,000! Not only does the use of leverage allow you to make a higher return off of each of your properties, but it also allows you to spread your investment dollars over many more properties. This *diversification* spreads the risk out and decreases the likelihood that any one investment can wipe you out financially.

Notice that so far we have considered your return based on income, but there is more to it than that. What happens to your return on investment when your properties go up in value over time?

Imagine that your $100,000 property is appreciating in value at the rate of five percent per year, a realistic rate of appreciation. Further imagine that you hold the property for five years before selling it. What is your return on investment from appreciation?

After five years the property is worth approximately $127,600 ($100,000 increasing at 5 percent per year for five years). Assuming selling expenses of $7,600 you will have "netted" $20,000 after the sale ($27,600 appreciation minus $7,600 selling expenses = $20,000 net). By dividing the $20,000 over five years we see that you netted $4,000 per year from appreciation. Since you only put down $10,000 to start, your $4,000 worth of appreciation amounts to a 40 percent annual return on investment due to appreciation ($4,000 is 40 percent of $10,000)!

You made 40 percent a year due to appreciation and, as we have already seen, you made 37 percent a year due to positive income. Add the two together and you had an annual return on investment of 77 percent per year! If we look at your return over the entire five-year period instead of on an annual basis the numbers look even more dramatic.

If you held the property for five years and made appreciation of $4,000 a year, your total appreciation was $20,000. If you made $3,700 a year in income, your total income was $18,500. So, over five years you made a total of $38,500 on an initial investment of $10,000. That is a 385 percent return on investment over five years! That sure beats a savings account that might return 8 to 15 percent (total, not per year) in interest over five years.

Your ability to use leverage to invest in real estate greatly magnifies your returns, and dramatically decreases the time it will take you to achieve your financial goals. Using the techniques you will learn later on in the book, I will teach you how to boost your returns to well over 400 percent in even less time than our example above.

You might wonder why it is so easy to use leverage to buy real estate—why are lenders so ready to lend money for real estate investments? Well, the same factors that make real estate such a good investment for you makes it a relatively safe bet for lenders. They understand the income generating ability of real estate, and this gives them some sense of confidence that borrowers will be able to make loan payments. They also understand that the intrinsic value of real estate will allow them to sell the property and get most or all of their money back if a borrower defaults on a loan. Either way, lenders see real estate as a relatively safe bet.

The fact that lenders are eager to make real estate loans

should serve as proof to you that real estate truly is a good investment. If lenders thought it was too risky they would not be so eager to lend.

Another factor making real estate such a good personal wealth creation vehicle is the favorable tax treatment it enjoys. Some of the tax benefits you will enjoy as a real estate investor include:

- Closing costs offset future capital gains;
- You can deduct the interest payments on your mortgages;
- You can deduct your local property taxes;
- Operating expenses are deductible;
- The annual depreciation expense allows you to "defer" taxes on a portion of your rental income until you sell, which boosts your current cash flow;
- Profits on the sale of real estate that is held for more than a year are taxed using "capital gains" rates, which are much lower than personal income tax rates;
- You can defer capital gains taxes by taking advantage of special "1031 Exchange" rules.

The cumulative effects of all of these tax benefits can be quite substantial with respect to your bottom line. Every dollar saved as the result of a favorable tax benefit is an extra dollar in your pocket! While it is not the purpose of this book to go into every nuance of the tax law with respect to real estate investing, it is important that we get into it just a little. Once you have a basic understanding you will be able to ask the right questions of your accountant or tax advisor.

First of all, the *costs* incurred by you in purchasing your properties can be used to offset any future capital gains (This is called "adjusting the basis," and is something that you should discuss with your tax advisor.) Included are such things as attorney fees, title insurance, lender fees, inspections, appraisals, surveys, etc. Purchasing a property can be thought of in the same light as purchasing a business.

The *interest* on your real estate loans is also deductible. A peculiar aspect of a standard "amortized" real estate loan is that although the payments remain constant over the life of the loan (we are assuming a fixed rate mortgage) the payment is actually being split between two different things, one being interest and the other being principal.

Interest is the fee a lender charges for lending money, and principal is an actual repayment of the money borrowed. If your friend lends you $100 for a year at 10 percent interest, at the end of the year you will have to pay her $110, which consists of $10 in interest and $100 of principal.

With most mortgages, whenever you make a mortgage payment, a portion goes to paying the interest on the loan and a portion goes to actually paying off the loan itself. But there is more to it than that. Not only is a portion of the overall payment being allocated to either principal or interest, but also the actual amounts allocated shifts over time. In the beginning years most of the payment is applied towards interest, with only a little going towards principal. In the later years most of the payment goes towards principal, with only a little going towards interest. It might sound odd, but that is the way it works.

Imagine that you have a thirty-year mortgage with payments of $800 per month. In the early years, perhaps $700 is going towards the payment of interest and $100 is going towards the payment of principal. However, over time the allocation shifts, so that in the later years perhaps only $100 of each payment is going towards interest with the rest now going towards principal.

If you think about it, this makes perfect sense. Every time you make a payment, the amount of money you still owe goes down a little. Since you now owe a little less money, the dollar amount of interest you are charged on the next payment goes down a little. Since your total payment amount remains constant over the life of the loan, the amount going towards interest goes down just a little bit with each payment and the amount going towards principal goes up.

So, what is the point of explaining all of this? As a real estate investor, the interest you pay on a mortgage is a deductible business expense. Since most of your mortgage payments will be going towards interest, the amount of money that you can deduct ends up being quite large. As you already know, the more money you can deduct, the more money you can save on taxes, and the more money you get to put in your pocket.

While not precisely accurate, a good rule of thumb is that in the earlier years of an amortized loan roughly 10.5 payments out of 12 will have gone towards interest, with the remaining 1.5 payments having gone towards principal. Going back to our $800 per month example, that means you would get to deduct about $8,400 as a business expense ($800/month x 10.5 months). Depending on your tax bracket, this deduction alone could end up saving you up to $3,000 at the end of the year!

Taxes paid on your investment properties are also considered business expenses and as such, can be deducted. Other deductions include all of the legitimate expenses you might encounter as a property owner. Such things as insurance, water and sewer, trash and snow removal, gas and electric, advertising, legal fees, bookkeeping, supplies, routine maintenance, etc. Any cost legitimately incurred in owning and operating your real estate investments is deductible. Smart investors keep track of every penny.

The tax laws allow real estate investors to *depreciate* their residential investment properties over a period of 27.5 years, and nonresidential properties over a period of 39 years. The word "depreciate" literally means "to loose value," and the tax authorities have recognized that nothing lasts forever, not even buildings. The depreciation expense is a way for investors to account for the fact that properties slowly wear out over time. You should be aware of the fact that land itself is never depreciated, but only the improvements to the land (buildings, fences, sewers, etc.)—only the man-made stuff.

Let's look at an example. Suppose that you have just purchased a residential investment property for $100,000. How much would you be able to write off as an annual depreciation expense? Since only structures are depreciated, the first thing that you have to do is determine how much of the $100,000 comes from the sale of the land and how much comes from the value of the improvements. For the sake of argument, let's say that the land is worth $20,000 and the improvements are worth $80,000.

We have already said that this is a residential property, so you know that its improvement value can be depreciated over a period of 27.5 years. Simply take the improvement value of $80,000 and divide it by 27.5 years. For this particular property you can take an annual depreciation expense of $2,909 ($80,000 divided by 27.5).

What if this property was nonresidential? Assuming the same purchase price, land value, and improvement value, the calculation is simple. Instead of dividing $80,000 by 27.5, you will divide it by the 39-year period allowed for nonresidential properties. You would be able to take an annual depreciation expense of $2,051 ($80,000 divided by 39).

You can see that the tax laws allow investors to depreciate residential properties faster than nonresidential properties, which means that the amount of annual depreciation expense that can be written off is larger for residential properties than it is for similarly valued nonresidential properties.

Understand that the depreciation expense is not a real expense that you have to pay out of your pocket like you do for such things as taxes, insurance, etc. Think of the depreciation expense as a phantom expense, the sole purpose of which is to allow you to decrease the amount of income that you have to claim for tax purposes.

Finally, understand that properties do not really lose all of their value after either 27.5 or 39 years—these are completely arbitrary numbers used only for tax purposes. The good thing is that this particular fantasy happens to be a good thing for real estate investors. While the rules with respect to depreciation are a bit more complicated than I have gone over here, now you know the basics. Once you get involved in real estate investing, your best bet is to have an accountant go over your taxes to make sure that you have fully taken advantage of all of the rules.

Whenever you decide to sell one of your properties, any gain that you make on the sale may be subject to the capital gains tax. Roughly speaking, capital gain is the difference between the cost of a property and the net amount made on its sale.

For tax purposes, the cost of a property is calculated by taking the amount spent to acquire it (initial price plus closing costs) adding in any money spent on capital improvements (new roof, new driveway, new boiler, etc.) and subtracting any depreciation you have taken. The amount made on the sale would be the sale price less any sales costs.

Tax rates applied to long-term capital gains are significantly less than the tax rates applied to personal income (since rates change periodically, I will not mention specific rates here). This is another reason why investors have an advantage over employees—dollar for dollar employees pay more taxes than investors!

While you will still pay personal income tax rates for the income generated by your investments, a significant portion of the money you make (probably as much as half, or more) will come from capital gains, which will be taxed at the lower rates.

At this point, I want to ask you a question. Even though capital gains tax rates are lower than personal income tax rates, if given the choice, would you rather not pay capital gains tax when you sell? Silly question? I suspect that you would rather not pay the tax if given the choice.

Well, believe it or not there is a choice! It is called the "Section 1031" exchange, also sometimes called a "Like Kind Exchange," or a "Starker Exchange" (The rule is found in "Section 1031" of the tax code. "Starker" was the guy who first tested the rule in court and won. "Like-kind" refers to the type of property involved).

Using a 1031 Exchange allows an investor to *defer* the payment of capital gains tax on the sale of a property, so long as certain rules are followed. Basically, it works like this. An investor identifies another piece of "Like Kind" property that he would like to own ("Like Kind" means any kind of real estate for any other kind of real estate. It could be a condo for a piece of raw land, but not a condo for a truck). Once the exchange property is identified, the investor purchases it with the proceeds from the sale of his property. That said, certain rules must be followed in order for the exchange to be considered legitimate in the eyes of the taxman.

First, the exchange property has to be identified within the first 45-days after the closing of the sold property. Next, the closing on the exchange property must take place within 180-days of the closing of the sold property. Finally, the investor must not have taken possession of the proceeds of the sale at any time between the time of the closings on the sold and identified properties.

The rules are strictly enforced. If the exchange property is identified later than 45 days from the closing on the sold property, the exchange will not be recognized by the taxman. If the purchase of the exchange property closes later than 180 days from the closing of the sold property, the exchange will not be recognized by the taxman. If the investor (or an agent of the investor, such as his attorney, accountant, or even a friend or family member) ever takes possession of the money, the exchange will not be recognized by the taxman.

You are probably wondering what happens to the money

from the investor's sale if neither he, his attorney, his accountant, nor anyone even associated with him can take the money. There are special companies called "Exchange Intermediaries" that hold the money in escrow during the time between the closing on the sold and identified proper-ties. A check is cut to the intermediary at the closing of the sold property and the intermediary cuts a check for the closing of the exchange property—the investor never sees the money during this period.

So long as *all* of the capital gain from the sale of a prop-erty is put into an exchange property, no capital gains tax is due. If only a portion of the capital gain is put into an exchange property, then only the tax on that portion will be deferred—tax will be due on the portion not put into the exchange property.

Understand that payment of the capital gain tax is only *deferred*; it is not eliminated. The amount of money deferred from taxation will be rolled into the capital gain when the exchange property is itself eventually sold.

If the capital gain when the exchange property is eventu-ally sold amounts to $100,000, and a gain of $50,000 was rolled into the property when it was initially purchased, then the capital gains tax due will be on $150,000—the total of the two. That said, you could roll the $150,000 gain into another exchange property, thus deferring the tax once again. As long as you keep doing 1031 Exchanges you will be able to defer paying capital gains taxes.

A natural question is, "Why bother deferring the capital gain if you are going to have to pay it eventually anyway?" The answer is simple—every dollar you don't have to give the taxman today is a dollar you can use to make more money with. Think about it. If you pay the taxman $10,000 today, then that $10,000 is gone to you forever. However, if you get to keep the $10,000 then you have the opportunity to buy another property that will generate even more income and capital gains for you.

Even though you eventually have to pay the capital gains tax, the extra money you get to make by deferring its payment far and away exceeds any extra taxes you might pay in the future. Many investors have used this technique to continually expand their real estate holdings from a few small investment houses to a large portfolio of investment buildings in a relatively short period of time.

Finally, I want to stress that the preceding discussion of taxes was merely intended to give you a general overview of some of the potential tax benefits of real estate investing. INDIVIDUAL TAX SITUATIONS VARY. DO NOT CONSIDER THIS BOOK TO BE A DEFINITIVE TREATMENT OF THE TAX CONSEQUENCES OF REAL ESTATE INVESTING. ALWAYS CONSULT WITH A COMPETENT TAX ADVISOR REGARDING YOUR PESONAL TAX SITUATION.

Your eyes have been opened to the lies and half-truths put out by the powers that be with regards to what it takes to get ahead financially. After all, if the propaganda were true then everybody would be rich!

It is time to cut through the lies, and to begin to learn a simple, proven, relatively inexpensive approach to controlling assets, generating income, and locking in profits. You will learn how to apply a step-by-step approach to investing that will virtually guarantee your success!

You will learn why SINGLE-FAMILY HOUSES ARE THE

VERY BEST ASSETS for beginning investors to invest in (and why many experienced investors continue to invest in them) and you will learn how to control these assets for only pennies on the dollar. You will learn how to virtually *eliminate the hassles of being a landlord* and virtually *eliminate risk*. And how to *lock-in profits of over 400 percent!* Are you ready? Then welcome to the *WealthLoop* system. . .

# Part II

# Chapter 5

## An Overview of the WealthLoop™ System

Your best chance of securing personal wealth for yourself and your family is to IMMEDIATELY begin investing in nice single-family houses in good neighborhoods. Why single-family houses? Because everybody wants one!

How many people do you know that do not want a house of their own? Chances are, nobody. Go into a room full of renters and ask them to raise their hand if they would like to own a house of their own. What percentage do you think would raise their hands? I guarantee you that 99 percent of those renters would raise their hand, but equally true is that most of them feel that for one reason or another the door to homeownership is blocked to them.

What if you knew how to give those renters exactly what they wanted? What if you had an affordable way to sell houses to renters who desperately wanted to own? Do you think that you could build a profitable niche for yourself? Do you think you could get rich?

The *WealthLoop* system is a proven approach to buying nice single-family houses in nice neighborhoods where people want to live, and then selling them on a "rent-to-own" basis to tenants who are dying to own a house of their own. Not only will you be providing a valuable and honorable service, but you will also be following a virtually foolproof plan for creating personal wealth for yourself.

The *WealthLoop* system will enable you to:

- Find exactly the right types of properties and buy them for a price that virtually assures that you make a large profit!

- Identify, attract, and pre-screen the types of tenants that will take care of your properties for you!

- Virtually eliminate the typical hassles of being a landlord by structuring your leases so that your tenants pay for most repairs!

- Lock-in profits of over 400 percent on every single-family house that you buy, and do it over and over again using your tenants' money!

- Start with just one house and turn it into as many as twenty houses in as little as 18 to 60 months!

- Generate hundreds, even thousands of dollars a month in positive cash flow!

- Start with just a few thousand dollars and turn it into tens, even hundreds of thousands of dollars of personal profit when you sell (this is above and beyond the monthly positive cash flow you will be generating)!

You will learn all of this and more. Our goal is to have you truly understand the system—to have you "feel it in your bones!"

The *WealthLoop* system is not a get rich quick scheme. It is a simple and steady approach to building wealth using proven techniques and sound principles of investing. I am going to teach you how to start slowly, but once you master the steps involved you might decide to ramp-up quickly in order to accelerate your wealth-building program. The choice of how quickly to proceed will be yours.

Many investors are content to purchase one to three properties a year indefinitely, but I know of one investor who purchased nearly twenty properties and quit his job after only one year using these techniques!

As you begin to learn and use these techniques remember your goal. Your goal is to create financial independence for you and your family. Your goal is to create a perpetual money machine. Your goal is to create a personal *Wealth-Loop*. Remember our definition:

"A *WealthLoop* is a series of *automatic income streams,* that are *independent of your personal labor,* and that are *sufficient to maintain your chosen individual lifestyle indefinitely.*"

We will start by exploring why certain types of properties, and certain investment strategies, are better than others when you are first starting out. You will learn the right things to do, as well as the mistakes to avoid. We will review all of the numbers so that you will know exactly how to minimize your expenses and maximize your profits and cash flow.

We will discuss financing, appraisals, inspections, and attorneys. You will learn what paperwork you will need and how to make sure that you are well protected in your transactions. In short, you will learn everything you need to know to become wealthy in as little as two to five years!

Imagine that! If you have just a few thousand dollars in

your pocket (or can scrape it up) a mere thirty-six months from now you could possibly be completely financially independent! Are you ready? Do you want to learn how to do it? Okay, then turn the page . . .

# Chapter 6

## How NOT to Get Started!

In my opinion, and as proven time and again by countless investors, the best way to start yourself on the road to financial independence is to start investing in single-family houses. A main reason why I recommend houses in the beginning is that houses are something that most people can already relate to, and for which they already have some degree of familiarity.

Think about it. How much do you know about the operation of apartment buildings? What do you know about strip malls? Office buildings? Houses are essentially simple structures with simple systems. They are easy to understand, operate and maintain.

For example, consider the types of tenants that are attracted to apartments and the types of tenants that are attracted to houses. Apartment renters tend to be more transient, less stable, and quite frankly, more of a pain in the neck to deal with.

Having worked with many building buyers and sellers over the years, I have heard countless horror stories from apartment building owners. Apartment tenants often do not get along with their neighbors. They are more prone to tearing up the property, leaving trash lying around, and skipping out on their lease without notifying the owner. Often times you have roommate and boyfriend/girlfriend situations that can lead to all sorts of problems.

Of course, I am making a generalization that does not hold true for all tenants or all building owners. Lest I have all of the apartment tenants in the world come after me, I fully admit there are many great apartment tenants out there. My point is simply that apartment buildings are statistically more difficult to own and manage than are single-family houses.

I am not saying that you should never invest in apartment buildings. I am simply saying that I believe single-family houses to be a better way to go for the *beginning* investor. While apartment buildings have proven to be fantastic investments for many owners, I also know of quite a few beginning investors who got in over their heads by investing in apartment buildings without having the requisite experience to handle them. In my opinion it is better to start with something simple, which investing in houses allows you to do.

Another reason why houses are the way to start out are the very favorable financing options available. Lenders for nonresidential properties and apartment buildings almost always require a borrower to make at least a 20 percent down-payment, and sometimes as much as 25 or 30 percent. Lenders for these types of properties also tend to scrutinize the borrower's financial criteria and real estate investing experience more so than for residential borrowers.

In contrast, residential loan programs tend to be much

more liberal in terms of the qualification criteria used to approve the loan, and depending on the borrower's credit scores, down-payment amounts of only 10 percent are very common, and can go as low as five or even zero percent down. Furthermore, residential loan interest rates are often one-half to two percent lower than rates charged for nonresidential loans.

Finally, there is greater demand for housing than for strip malls or offices. Everybody needs a place to live but not everybody needs retail or office space. The vacancy rates for residential properties have historically been much lower than for other types of properties. It is simply easier to find tenants for houses than for other types of properties.

Allowing for the fact that investing in houses is the easiest, cheapest, safest, and fastest way to invest in real estate, let's take a look at the numbers . . .

# Chapter 7

## The Economics of Single-Family Houses

Here is a typical rundown of how the numbers might look (assuming tenants pay all of their own utilities) for a $100,000 investment property purchased with a 10% down payment, and a 30-year amortized mortgage at 7% interest:

| | |
|---|---|
| Purchase Price: | $100,000 |
| Down Payment: | $ 10,000 |
| Loan Amount: | $ 90,000 |
| | |
| Monthly Loan Payment: | $ 599 |
| Monthly Property Tax Payment: | $ 200 |
| Monthly PMI*: | $ 60 |
| Monthly Property Insurance: | $ 40 |
| Water/sewer: | $ 50 |
| Total Monthly Payment: | $ 949 |
| | |
| Monthly Rental Income: | $ 1,050 |
| **Monthly Positive Cash Flow** | **$ 101** |

*PMI is an insurance fee that you pay if your down payment is less than 20% of the purchase price.

From the example you can see that if you had made the above investment you would have earned $101 per month on this property. I suspect that you might be thinking that $101 a month is not a lot of money. You might even be thinking that such an investment is not worth the effort.

Fortunately however, first looks can be very, very deceiving. In reality, this one little house is a money making machine in disguise!

The truth is that you would be accumulating a great deal more than $101 a month. You would actually be accumulating money and building wealth in four different ways:

1. **Monthly Cash Flow** – This is the $101 a month.

2. **Equity Build-Up** – Every month that your tenants make a loan payment for you the amount of your loan balance goes down a little and the amount of your equity goes up a little. Every dollar of increased equity is another dollar that belongs to you. Realize that the money to pay down the loan is coming from the tenant in the form of rent, which is why I said, "your tenant makes a loan payment for you." They are in effect buying the property, but you get to own it! The reality of this example is that in addition to the $101 of positive cash flow, you are accumulating another $75 a month in the form of equity build-up.

3. **Tax Benefit** – Remember the depreciation expense? You will be depreciating this property by taking a write-off on your personal income taxes. On a property like this you could possibly save about $1,000 annually. This is real money that would have been paid to the taxman, but that you get to keep just because you own investment property. The $1,000 tax savings comes out to about $83 a month in additional money to you.

**4. Appreciation** – As property values rise, so will the value of your investment property. Historically, a five percent increase in value for each year that you own the property is not unrealistic. The value of a $100,000 property will increase by $5,000 the first year and five percent every year thereafter. Dividing a $5,000 increase in value by twelve months comes to about $417 a month. This is real money that belongs to you.

So, let's take another look at this one little house that at first looked like it might not even be worth your time and effort:

| | |
|---|---|
| Monthly Cash Flow: | $101 |
| Monthly Equity Build-Up: | $ 75 |
| Monthly Tax Benefit: | $ 83 |
| Monthly Appreciation: | $417 |
| **Total Monthly Return:** | **$676** |

($8,112 annually)

Wow, this one little house that at first did not look like it would even be worth your effort turns out to be a tremendous little money machine after all, and the best part about it is that *most of the money is locked-up in the property*. Because you cannot immediately get your hands on most of this money, you will be building wealth whether you like it or not!

The only money that you will be able to get your hands on right away will be the $101 a month. While you might think that not having access to all of it immediately is a bad thing, in terms of creating wealth and attaining financial freedom this is a tremendous opportunity. Later we will look at how to use this locked up equity to buy house after house after house—all coming from your original $10,000 investment.

Imagine if you held onto this one little *money machine* for thirty years until the mortgage was paid off. No more mortgage payments means a large monthly cash flow for your retirement. Also, you would then own a free and clear asset worth $432,000 ($100,000 appreciating at five percent per year for 30 years). All of this from just one house and an initial investment of $10,000! Imagine if you had bought just three houses. Imagine if you had bought ten or twenty!

As you can see, single-family houses can serve as powerful wealth creation vehicles, but keep in mind that we have just been looking at the numbers in general terms. As we delve deeper into the *WealthLoop* system you will learn techniques and strategies to increase your returns well beyond what we have looked at thus far.

# Chapter 8

## The Right Way to Invest in Houses

I have shown you why investing is the only realistic approach to personal wealth creation for the average man or woman, and I have explained why it is my fervent belief that real estate is the safest and most practical investing option for most people.

We looked at the various reasons why investing in single-family houses is an easier, safer, and less expensive way for beginners to get started in real estate, and finally we looked at the economics of investing in houses and found the numbers to be quite impressive. Now let's discuss the two primary strategies of house investors and show how the *WealthLoop* system combines the best from both strategies into a superior investing approach.

As an investor, you could choose either a *buy and hold* approach or a *buy and flip* approach to buying houses. The *buy and hold* approach is just what it sounds like. You buy a property, become a landlord, and rent the property to tenants. The *buy and flip* approach is where you buy a property below market value and quickly resell it for more money than it cost you, thus quickly getting back your initial investment, plus hopefully, a tidy profit.

As a *buy and hold* investor you would be making money in the four ways we discussed earlier:

1. Monthly Cash Flow
2. Equity Build-Up
3. Tax Benefit
4. Appreciation

As we saw when we reviewed the numbers earlier, this is a great way to amass wealth. With just a few properties you could do quite well for yourself. However, as with anything in life, there are some not so fun aspects of the *buy and hold* approach that you would have to deal with.

First, tenants can be challenging. They are not likely to care for the property as you would, and when they move out they might leave the place in poor shape. This will cost you time and expenses in getting the property ready to re-rent—the cost of the repairs themselves plus the lost rental income during the time you are getting the unit back in shape.

Some tenants can be very trying on your nerves. It is not unusual to get calls at odd hours—toilets break at 2:00 a.m., people get locked out of their apartments, garage doors get stuck. One building owner I know told me a story about one lady who would call him whenever one of her light bulbs burned out!

I am not telling you that being a landlord is bad. *Many investors have made a fortune as landlords and perhaps you will too one day.* I just want you to know that with all of the good, there are hassles and frustrations to be dealt with on a regular basis if you decide to go the *buy and hold* route. I have designed the *WealthLoop* system to minimize or eliminate the hassles and expenses generally associated with the *buy and hold* approach.

Now let's take a look at the *buy and flip* approach. As a *buy and flip* investor you would be making money from only one source—the difference between what it cost you to buy, hold, fix up and sell the property, and the price you got for the property when you sold it.

With this approach, you have to buy the property well below market value, which is not as easy as it sounds. Everybody is looking for a great deal. Not only are you competing against other investors, but also real estate agents themselves, who often buy the best deals before they ever hit the general market.

Remember that people are not in the habit of "giving away" their properties. If you do manage to find a property for sale at what you consider to be a below market value price, there is a high likelihood that the property is in need of significant upgrades and/or repairs. In that case you either need to be an expert yourself or hire an expert at evaluating the condition of properties and estimating the costs of repair, remembering that a slip-up here could eat up most or all of your expected profits.

A *buy and flip* investor also has to be very familiar with the exact neighborhood he is considering buying in. Many would-be "flippers" have gotten burned when they finally realized that what they thought they could sell their property for was nothing close to what the market was actually willing to pay. Success as a *buy and flip* investor requires knowledge and skills that most beginning investors simply do not have.

Of course, I am not saying that the *buy and flip* approach is bad. *Many investors have made fortunes using this method and perhaps you will too one day.* The upside to the *buy and flip* approach to investing (if you do it right) is that you eliminate the hassles of landlording, and you get your initial investment back fairly quickly. This is a great way to make money in real estate but a very risky approach for the *inexperienced* investor. I have designed the *WealthLoop* system to incorporate the upside benefits of the *buy and flip* approach while minimizing or eliminating the downside.

So what are the benefits from each approach that we want to retain, and what are the downside elements we want to avoid?

| Benefits to Retain | Downsides to Avoid |
|---|---|
| **Buy and Hold Approach** | |
| Cash flow | Unexpected repair costs |
| Equity build-up | High tenant turnover |
| Tax benefit | Hassles of landlording |
| Appreciation | Tenants don't care about the property |
| **Buy and Flip Approach** | |
| Fairly quick return of initial investment | Need extensive knowledge |
| Eliminate responsibility for ongoing repairs | Need extensive experience |
| Eliminate hassles of being a landlord | |

An ideal approach would incorporate the best of both approaches, which is exactly what the *WealthLoop* system manages to do. The *WealthLoop* approach allows you to profit from all four avenues of wealth creation (cash flow, equity build-up, tax benefit, and appreciation) but as you will learn, you will quickly recoup most or all of your initial investment by securing a fifth income stream: the "upfront" payment.

The *WealthLoop* system allows you to avoid the most onerous hassles of landlording and places responsibility for most repairs in the hands of your tenants. It also allows you to lock in your profits up front.

So, how do we accomplish this best-of-both-worlds outcome? The secret to the *WealthLoop* system is that it allows you to capitalize on the intrinsic demand for certain types of real estate by certain types of tenant/buyers. You will be providing a highly sought-after service, and because you are providing this service to people who would not be able to own their own home if it were not for your help, you will be richly and fairly rewarded. This is a win-win for all concerned!

In a nutshell, you will be finding and buying nice single-family houses in decent neighborhoods and selling them under a short-term "rent to own" program to a tenant/buyer. You will structure the transaction so that it is a win-win for everybody concerned: you make money, the bank makes money, and tenants who might not have had the opportunity to own their own home become homeowners. It is a noble path to real estate investing that actually helps other people to achieve their dream of homeownership while at the same time virtually assuring you a path to financial independence.

This system has proven itself to be extremely effective at generating wealth and it virtually eliminates most of the risks and hassles associated with real estate investing. You can do this!

Selling properties on a rent to own basis is a simple

enough concept to grasp, and sales of this type are not uncommon. In fact, the first property I bought in Chicago was on a rent to own basis. I saw an ad in the paper that said, "Rent to Own" and I called (see how easy and effective the advertising for this type of sale is). I was in law school, so I was not working, but the owner saw me as a good risk and we did the deal.

Twenty-eight months later I closed on the property. It was a win for me because I was able to buy a nice property at a time when I would not have qualified for conventional bank financing, and it was a win for the seller because he sold his property at a fair price.

For the investor, rent-to-own programs basically work like this:

1. You find a nice property in a decent neighborhood and buy it.
2. You find a tenant that would like to own his or her own home.
3. You sign a lease with your tenant for two to three years. (Actually, it could be for as long or as short as you want, but two to three years is ideal.)
4. You make a separate agreement with the tenant that gives them the option to purchase the property for a pre-agreed price at any time during the lease period (This is why rent to own programs are often called "Lease-Options").

Of course, there are many details for structuring a lease option correctly—to maximize your returns and minimize your risks while making it attractive to prospective tenant/buyers. I will teach you all of the details in later chapters.

You will learn exactly how to attract good tenant/buyers and how to get the paperwork right. That said, before we go into the details of structuring deals, let's look at a general example of how the numbers might look. As we go through the example, please do not get distracted wondering how to make it happen. Concentrate on the big picture and know that the details will come later on when I show you how to put it all together.

To keep the numbers simple, let's assume that you found a great little house in a nice neighborhood that's worth $110,000. Because you know what to look for in selecting properties, you managed to purchase it for $100,000 with a 10 percent down payment. (This is actually quite easy to do—I will teach you techniques later for finding good deals.) Let's further assume that houses are appreciating at a historically realistic five percent per year and that you are going to lease-option the property to a tenant/buyer for two years. Appreciating at five percent per year, your $110,000 valued property will be worth $121,275 in two years. You set the two-year lease-option price with your tenant/buyer at $125,000.

Do you realize what you have just done? You purchased a $110,000 property for $100,000, which means you made 10 percent right off the bat. Then you pre-sold the property based on its future value, which earned you another 14 percent. You have already locked in a 24 percent profit, but it doesn't end there! The numbers look like this:

| | |
|---|---|
| Property Value: | $110,000 |
| Purchase Price: | $100,000 |
| Loan Amount: | $ 90,000 |
| Down Payment: | $ 10,000 |
| Closing Costs: | $ 2,000 |
| **Out Of Pocket Amount:** | **$ 12,000** |
| | |
| Monthly Loan Payment: | $ 599 |
| | |
| Monthly Property Tax Payment: | $ 200 |
| Monthly PMI: | $ 60 |
| Monthly Property Insurance: | $ 40 |
| Water/sewer | $ 50 |
| Total Monthly Payment: | $ 949 |
| Monthly Rental Income: | $ 1,250 |
| **Monthly Positive Cash Flow:** | **$ 301** |
| | |
| **Up-Front Payment From Tenant/Buyer:** | **$ 4,000** |

Now pay close attention to how this deal works itself out. You invested a down payment plus closing costs of $12,000 and within a few weeks of purchasing the property you get $4,000 back in the form of an up-front payment from your tenant/buyer. You are also getting a monthly positive cash flow of $301, equity build-up, and a tax benefit.

During the first year you are getting $3,612 in rental cash flow. You are also making about $75 a month from equity build-up due to your mortgage payments (that adds another $900). You save about $1,000 on your income taxes by virtue of the fact that you owned this property and were able to take a depreciation expense. Finally, do not forget the $4,000 up-front payment you received. You made $9,512 during the first year. You made this $9,512 on an initial investment of $12,000, which means that your first year return on investment is about 79 percent. In year two you will once again be making a positive cash flow of $3,612, an equity build-up of about $900, and a tax benefit of about $1,000, which totals $5,512 for the second year.

When the tenant buys the house, the numbers look like this:

| | | |
|---|---|---|
| Sale Price | $125,000 | |
| Less Up-front Payment Amount | $ 4,000 | |
| Less Total Monthly Rent Credits | $ 6,000 | (explained later) |
| Less Loan Payoff | $ 88,200 | (loan minus equity) |
| Net From Sale | $ 26,800 | |
| Plus Cash Flow | $ 7,224 | |
| Plus Up-Front Payment Received | $ 4,000 | |
| Plus Tax Benefit | $ 2,000 | |
| Total During Option Period | $ 40,024 | |

In 24-months you made $40,024 on an initial investment of $12,000. This equals a total return over two years of 334 percent! Where else are you going to get a return like that in two years? But just saying this does not fully illustrate how this approach truly minimized the amount of money you had at risk.

Yes, you put out $12,000 up front but you also got back $4,000 of it almost immediately, which means you really only had $8,000 in the pot after you rented the property. Add to this the fact that you got back another $3,612 in cash-flow, $900 in equity build-up, and $1,000 in tax benefit during the first year, and you can see that you only had $2,488 left in the pot after the first year (subtract the $5,512 worth of first year income streams that you got back from the $8,000 still in the pot at that point).

By year two, after only five and one-half months, you have gotten all of your money back. (Note: $5,512 per year equals $459.33 a month; at the beginning of the second year you only have $2,488 left in the pot; with $459.33 accruing every month, it only takes 5.42 months before you have made back that $2,488 back. In other words, you have accrued all of your money back in less than 18 months!)

Finally, remember that the less you put down, the higher your return. I do not want to beat a dead horse by going over the numbers again in detail, but suffice it to say that had you taken out a 95 percent loan and put down only five percent instead of 10 percent, your return on investment over the two years would be over 400 percent!

Are you getting a feel for how the whole thing works? Are you getting excited? You can do this! This is simple. I want you to understand the simplicity of the approach.

Yes, we have looked at the numbers, but the point is not to get bogged down in numbers or to turn into some sort of financial genius. The point of the example is for you to get a basic understanding of how the system works.

Once you get started buying houses using the *Wealth-Loop* system you will find that sometimes you will make more money than in these examples and sometimes you will make less. But tell me, are you really going to be upset if you get into a deal and only make 295 percent instead of 425 percent? In my opinion, this is the safest, simplest and most consistent approach to take. Again, DO NOT GET BOGGED DOWN THINKING YOU HAVE TO MASTER EVERY LAST DETAIL at this point. As we continue you will be learning exactly how to structure your transactions for ease, profit, and safety.

Ready to become financially free? Then turn the page. . .

# Chapter 9

## Now is Not the Time to Psyche Yourself Out!

At this point, many people decide to throw it all away before they even get started. They begin to talk themselves out of creating personal wealth and financial freedom, by rationalizing about all of the reasons why they think they might fail. They start saying things to themselves like:

- What if I can't find any tenants?
- What if I do find tenants, but they don't pay me?
- What if I buy a lemon and it starts to fall apart?
- What happens if the tenant doesn't buy the house at the end of the lease-option?
- Nobody is ever going to go for such a deal!
- I'll never get enough rent to cover my costs!
- It would be one thing if I already knew what I was doing, but it's too complicated for me to get started!

*Truth be told, the riskiest piece of real estate in the world is the six-inch piece of real estate between your ears!*

Far and away, the greatest risk you will face on the road to financial independence will be the risk of giving in to your fears and self-doubts. This is where we separate the men from the boys and the women from the girls, so before you begin to go down that road, let's look rationally at the answers to these self-defeating questions.

## What if I can't find any tenants?

You are going to be finding and purchasing NICE houses in NICE neighborhoods. These are the types of houses that the average working man and woman can afford, and that they would be proud to come home to and proud to own, so why in the world would you not be able to rent your property?

There are only four possible reasons why a property would sit vacant for any length of time:

1) It is not being marketed/advertised properly;
2) It's a lousy property;
3) It's in a lousy neighborhood;
4) It's priced too high.

Those are the only possible reasons for a prolonged vacancy.

In later chapters you will learn exactly how to find the right types of properties in desirable areas. We will also show you the exact ads to use to attract highly motivated tenant/buyers. Assuming you follow what we teach, there can only be one reason for you ever having a prolonged vacancy.

Here is a BIG secret. If you are ever having trouble renting a property—DROP THE ASKING RENT 50 BUCKS! If you still cannot rent it—DROP IT ANOTHER 50 BUCKS! Look, sometimes you will make a few hundred a month in cash flow and sometimes only $75, BUT SO WHAT? You already know that the real money comes from the appreciation, tax benefit, up-front payment, and equity build-up.

Even if you only made $0.00 a month in positive cash flow, would that really be so terrible? You would still be getting all of the other income streams (appreciation, tax benefit, up-front payment, and equity build-up) and your tenant/buyers would still be covering the expenses—they would be buying the house for you, for free! Think about it. As long as you can cover the payments for a few weeks until the property is rented, you have almost no downside. This concern is really a fantasy. Stop worrying about it!

## What if I do find tenants but they don't pay me?

This could happen, but how likely is it and would it really be such a terrible thing? Remember that the *WealthLoop* system is a rent-to-own program that protects the investor by either greatly reducing or completely eliminating the majority of risks normally associated with real estate investing.

First, tenant/buyers typically have a much different attitude than the standard tenant. They will eventually own the property, which means that they have a lot at stake and tend to be MUCH more conscientious about making the rent payments. Later in the book you will learn special techniques for setting up your leases to create HUGE incentives for your tenant/buyers to pay on time.

Also, we will show you how to willingly and enthusiastically have your tenant/buyers pay you anywhere from three to five percent of your selling price as an up-front payment towards their eventual purchase. Even if one of your tenant/buyers did happen to default on their agreement, the up-front payment will serve as a solid financial cushion to support you until you can evict the tenant/buyer and get a new tenant/buyer into the property.

By using the *WealthLoop* system you will most likely come out ahead financially even if you do have to evict a tenant/buyer, and you would find yourself in a much better position than the conventional landlord in a similar situation! Yes, evicting a tenant is a bit of a hassle, but it happens everyday and it is just one of those things that has to be done sometimes. It is a VERY RARE but fairly routine part of being involved in real estate—get used to it.

While your current inexperience might cause you to be frightened by the possibility of having to evict a tenant/buyer someday, the reality is that the *WealthLoop* system minimizes the likelihood of this ever happening, and with experience you will come to realize that it is not such a big deal anyway. This is another fear that isn't worth getting all worked up about!

### What if I buy a "lemon" and the house starts falling apart?

Why would you ever buy a lemon? We will give you a checklist so that you know EXACTLY what to look for and what to avoid. We will teach you to NEVER buy a house without having a certified property inspector perform an inspection, so that you know about all of the issues that might be of concern with respect to a particular property.

We will teach you how to get the person you are buying the property from to provide a home warranty for all of the major systems in the property (plumbing, electrical, appliances, etc.). Here's the bottom line: if you don't buy junk, it won't fall apart!

Finally, you will learn how to set up your leases so that your tenant/buyers are responsible for virtually all repairs. Here again, this is a problem that turns out to be not much of a problem at all.

## What if the tenant doesn't buy the house after all?

In this case you would end up having the opportunity to make even more money and an even higher rate of return. Let's be clear, you really do want your tenant/buyers to buy your properties at the end of their lease-option periods, but the reality is that if your tenant/buyers decide not to buy their property you will actually make more money, because then you can go ahead and lease-option to a new tenant/buyer at a higher inflation-adjusted price.

Helping people who could not otherwise achieve home ownership without your assistance entails its own rewards. Everything in life is not about making money. However, a lease-option is just that—an option. It gives the tenant/buyer the option but not the obligation to buy the property. Things change. Family situations change. Career situations change. It is possible that a tenant/buyer may choose not to exercise their option to purchase, but this should be no cause of alarm to you. You would simply go ahead and find another tenant/buyer for the property.

It is true that if a tenant buyer decides not to exercise their option they will lose any up-front payments and rental credits that they may have accrued. But that is their decision, not yours. Later in the book you will see how to structure your rent-to-own program so that everything is clearly spelled out up front. We will get to the details later, but take my word for it that there is no problem here worthy of worrying about.

## Nobody is ever going to go for such a deal!

Says who? Everyday, transactions are structured using the techniques you are learning now. The type of people who will ultimately become your tenant/buyers are good solid people who, for one reason or another, are not able to get conventional bank financing to buy a home. Without your help these people would most certainly not be able to achieve their dream of home-ownership. The people who don't understand this arrangement are not the ones you want to deal with anyway. The good prospects will recognize the opportunity you are giving them and take you up on it.

They understand the up-front payment that they make is toward their eventual purchase. They know that if they buy the property they will get a 100 percent credit towards their purchase price, and if they choose not to buy the property, the up-front payment is considered additional rent that is not refunded.

The up-front money serves two purposes. First, it gives you a cushion for taking a risk on somebody who has less than perfect credit but on whom you are willing to take a chance—and believe me, they will appreciate the opportunity you are giving them. Secondly, and most importantly, the up-front money requirement weeds out the bad candidates and the not-so-serious prospects.

One of the reasons that you are willing to take a chance on these tenant/buyers is that they are proving themselves to be taking charge of their finances by having been able to come up with the up-front payment in the first place. The last thing that you want is a tenant/buyer who cannot come up with any money! The fact that they are putting down money up-front, with the full understanding that they will not get a refund if they decide not to exercise their option, means that they are very, very serious.

You will be amazed at how easy it is to find this type of tenant buyer. While there are always exceptions to a rule, in general you will find that this type of tenant/buyer tends to be very grateful for the opportunity, takes very good care of the property, and will generally be an ideal tenant that will give you very little trouble.

The *WealthLoop* system is set up to make finding and screening prospective tenant/buyers a simple process that attracts more than enough good candidates for each property. For every property you advertise you will probably have to turn several good candidates away, which is a great motivation for you to go out and find more properties to buy!

## I'll never get enough rent to cover my costs!

Why not? Before you ever buy a property you are going to find out exactly what the going rental rates for similar properties in the area are. This is simple enough to do—just drive around the neighborhood and look for any For Rent signs and call them, look in the newspaper and call on ads for similar properties, and call a few property management companies and ask them how much rents are going for in the area.

Although I did not yet come right out and say it, one of the beauties of the *WealthLoop* system is that you will UNDOUBTEDLY be able to charge a premium of 15 to 25 percent above going rental rates for a given area and have your tenant/buyers be more than willing to pay it.

How? Simply put, the people for whom this program is a great opportunity are those that have made financial mistakes in the past but who are on track in getting their act together and are looking for a way to get their credit back in order. These are people whose past actions preclude them from obtaining bank financing.

From the tenant/buyer's point of view, there are two MAJOR benefits to working with a seller using the *Wealth-Loop* system: 1) they have an opportunity to purchase a home of their own when other avenues have been closed to them due to their past financial mistakes and misfortunes, and 2) they have a built-in savings mechanism that virtually guarantees that they will be able to accumulate the funds to be able to purchase the property—if they stay on track.

Put yourself in their shoes. If you had poor credit but were motivated and on track to getting your "financial house in order," would you take this deal:

> *"Here's the deal Joe and Nancy. I will sell you this house today, but we don't have to close on the sale for three years, which will give you plenty of time to save the money you will need to buy it. To make the deal fair for both of us, the price will be $xxx,xxx, which is today's value plus normal appreciation over the three years.*
>
> *I understand your current financial situation, so*

*here is what we are going to do to make this happen for you. The current rental rate for a property like this one is $1,100 a month. But since you want to buy the property let's structure it this way: the rent will be $1,375 a month, which is $275 more than the current going rate.*

*Out of the extra $275 a month, $225 will be a 100 percent credit against the purchase price, so at the end of the three years you will have saved $8,100 in the form of a full credit. The other $50 a month is a small bit of extra rent that I get for taking a chance on you, and keeping the property off the market for three years. As we already discussed, you will need to give me an up-front payment, which will also be fully credited to you when we close on the sale in three years.*

*So, Joe and Nancy, I am willing to take a chance on you. If you are not 100 percent serious about buying the property I suggest that you don't do it. If you back out of the deal, not only do you lose out on a chance to own a home but your up-front money and rental credits will be considered extra rent and will not be refunded. You have to really want me to help you, and you have to be really serious about getting your finances in order and purchasing your own home."*

If you were in Joe and Nancy's position what would you do? The fact is that this is a very fair deal for them. You are helping them save their money and get their credit in order. In this example, they get a full credit for all but $50 a month, which is more than fair considering the break you are giving them—if you wanted, you could forgo the extra $50 and give them full credit for $275 (within the guidelines I am I teaching you, you can structure your deals anyway you want).

Furthermore, they will only loose their up-front money and rental credits if they back out of the deal, which is why everything is explained up-front and in writing. (Later in the book, you will learn exactly how to set up your agreements). You will find that there are many, many people willing to take a deal like this. Your problem is not going to be finding someone to take the deal but figuring out which prospective tenant/buyer to choose!

# Chapter 10

## Location + Size + Price + Curb Appeal = Success

Before you actually begin to look at properties, you have to do some research and find those areas that are appropriate for implementing the *WealthLoop* system. The system works best when applied to what I call "Bread and Butter" (B&B) properties. B&B properties are those that the average working man and woman would want to live in and can afford. Generally speaking, we are talking about houses with at least three bedrooms, one and one-half baths, a basement, and a garage, that are valued under $150,000.

Staying "below $150,000" is not a hard and fast rule but a guideline, because prices vary widely in different parts of the country. The point is that the property has to be affordable to most people in the area. You are not going after the million-dollar property market, you are going after the masses. (But hey, if you can make the system work in the upscale property market after you get some experience, then go for it.) By targeting the vast lower-middle and middle classes you can assure yourself of having the widest possible potential pool of tenant/buyers for your properties.

Location should be considered in tandem with price-range. You want to buy properties in nice, clean, safe, and respectable neighborhoods, neighborhoods that most people would find appealing. Obviously, given the desired price range, I am not suggesting that the neighborhoods need to be opulent or fancy, but they do have to have what those in the real estate business call "curb appeal." Look for neighborhoods where the streets are clean, houses are well kept, and the lawns are cut.

In my opinion and experience it is best to focus on HOUSES and avoid condominiums. A prime reason why the *WealthLoop* system works so well is that it allows people who could not do so otherwise to realize their *dream* of home ownership. While many people *dream* of the proverbial home with a white picket fence, few people *dream* of a condominium in a condo-complex where they have common walls with neighbors who they may not even get along with. The *American Dream* is a house in the suburbs, not a condo in a complex!

The *dream* is about SPACE! It is about room to grow, to live, and to relax. Always look for at least three bedrooms. Always look for more than one bath—two or more full baths is best, but one and one-half will do. Always look for a nice backyard. A basement is a must if you live in a part of the country where basements are common. I know, for example, that in many parts of the Southwest basements tend to be rare, so in that case don't worry about it. But if you live in the Chicago area, for example, a basement is a virtual must. Likewise, if garages are the norm in your part of the country, do not even consider a house without a garage. As a general rule of thumb, when it comes to implementing the *WealthLoop* system, the bigger the house the better!

In my own real estate brokerage business, when I first

started thinking about appropriate places for my beginning small investor clients to put their money, I set some rules with respect to what I would consider acceptable locations. First, I decided to keep the search area to within an hour's drive of Chicago (where we are located) my reasoning being that any more than that might become a hassle for all concerned. However, you should feel free to define your area according to whatever is comfortable for you. I know many, many people who operate in several states at once, so do not make too big a deal of this, but do keep in mind your tolerance for commuting as you are researching areas. As a general rule, beginning investors should stick to areas within a one-hour drive from home.

Besides distance, pay attention to the economics of the areas you are considering. During my own research with respect to the greater Chicago area I found several areas where one could find very nice three-bedroom houses with one and one-half baths, basements and garages for between $90,000 and $120,000. These were the exact kinds of properties I was looking for!

However, even though they contained the right kinds of properties, upon further research I realized that the economic conditions necessary to maintain a high demand for the properties varied considerably from community to community. Certain areas showed signs of an economic slow-down that had been ongoing for years. These areas were characterized by high vacancy rates, property foreclosures, and factory closings. In contrast, other areas showed clear signs of economic growth and vibrancy, with relatively low-vacancy rates, low foreclosure rates, and signs of business expansion—these are the kinds of areas you should be looking for.

Once you have done your research and defined the

areas you want to work in, it is time to start locating specific properties to look at. Locating properties can be done in several ways. You can hire a real estate agent/broker, you can surf numerous real estate web sites, you can drive around neighborhoods and look for "For Sale" and "For Rent" signs, you can call on classified ads, and you can run "Wanted To Buy" ads of your own.

By far, the least expensive, most accurate, easiest, and least time-consuming method of finding properties is to find and stick with a good real estate agent/broker. It is the least expensive method because it is absolutely free! The agent gets paid a buyer commission from the selling agent who listed the property. You do not have to pay your agent a dime.

It is the most accurate method, because real estate agents are wired into the system through their local multiple-listing service (MLS), which means they have real-time access to every single property that is listed by every single brokerage in their area. Having real-time access to all listed properties on the market is a very powerful tool that you should be taking advantage of as you search for properties.

Even the hundreds of real estate search web sites that are out there mostly pull their data from local MLS sites and incorporate it into their own sites. The experiences of both my clients and myself are that the information these sites provide often proves to be dated and incomplete. Why rely on secondhand, recycled MLS data when you can get real-time, up-to-the-minute information from your agent? The fact is that there is no more accurate source of local real estate listing information than a local real estate agent with access to the local MLS. Everything else is second best.

One last comment about working with real estate agents/brokers: find one or two good agents to work with and then stick with them! These people get paid on a commission basis, and then, only if they find you what you are looking for. How much time and effort do you think they are going to put into finding you properties if they know that you are talking to every real estate agent in town? If an agent is doing a bad job for you, then fire them! But as long as they are doing a good job for you, you should remain loyal to them.

An agent who knows that you are loyal to them and that you appreciate all of the free work they are doing for you, will bust his or her tail to actively hunt down properties that meet your criteria. A good agent who knows that you are being loyal to them may even go beyond the MLS and actively solicit owners of the types of properties you are looking for, even if they are not officially on the market. Such service means that you would have first crack at these properties before anyone else even knows that the owners are thinking of selling, which could lead to some great off-market deals for you. In the beginning talk to lots of agents, but once you find one or two who understand what you are trying to accomplish and who are willing to work hard for you, stick with them (I suggest that you give them a copy of this book to read, so that they know exactly what you are trying to do).

In addition to finding a good agent to do the majority of the research and running around for you, you might want to make it a regular practice to drive through the areas you are interested in to search for "For Sale" and "For Rent" signs. Take a pad of paper with you and jot down the addresses and telephone numbers of the properties you

are interested in. If the signs are from real estate companies give the information to your agent so that he/she can
get you the property info (this will keep you from having to
talk to 50 agents who are all trying to give you their sales
pitch). If you come across FSBO signs (pronounced "Fizz-
Bo", which stands for "For Sale By Owner") you can call
yourself, or you still might want to have your agent call on
your behalf.

Regarding calling on "For Rent" signs, you would be surprised at what a good source of potential purchases these
can be. You just might catch an owner who is sick and
tired of landlording the conventional way, and since very
few investors ever think to call on rental signs, you might
be able to negotiate a deal that's free from competition.
Once you get some experience under your belt you should
be able to negotiate directly with FSBO and rental sellers,
but while you are starting out, I would recommend that
you negotiate through your real estate agent. Negotiating a
real estate deal is not as easy as you might think, so it pays
to have an experienced player on your side. You might also
consider calling on the FSBO and rental ads in the local
newspaper for the areas you are interested in.

# Chapter 11

## Finding Good Deals and Picking Winners

You have done your research and have identified particular neighborhoods and communities that you want to invest in:

- The general economic conditions are stable and favorable;

- The right types of properties are available: three-bedroom houses with one and one-half baths, basements (if applicable), garages (if applicable), nice back yards, and priced under $150,000;

- The rents in the areas you have chosen are in line with what you would need to make a lease-option deal work for you and a tenant/buyer;

- The houses in your selected neighborhoods are well kept and have good curb-appeal.

Rather than having to look at every property on the market, the *WealthLoop* system gives you a set of guidelines for prioritizing your search so that you can concentrate your efforts on those properties most likely to be the best deals.

The cornerstone of the *WealthLoop* system is the use of what has been called a "10-5-10" investment strategy. The strategy itself is simple:

- Negotiate purchases for 10 percent below current market value.
- Borrow using five percent down payment (or less) investor loan programs.
- Pre-sell properties for at least 10 percent above current market values utilizing a rent-to-own selling system.

As you can see right off the bat, this strategy gives you a 20 percent profit spread between what you pay for the property and what you sell it for. You already know how to sell the property for at least 10 percent above its current market value to a tenant/buyer (you set up a two-year rent to own program, where the sale price assumes a five percent appreciation for each year over the two years). But you might not know how to negotiate a purchase price that is ten percent below the current market value. Surprisingly, it is much easier than you might think.

Notice that you do not have to negotiate huge discounts to be successful using the *WealthLoop* system. In fact, investment strategies that are based on you having to purchase properties at a steep discount to market value are almost always impractical and doomed to fail unless you are willing to dedicate a huge amount of time and effort to their implementation. Let's face it, how many people do you think are willing to give their property away for fifty cents on the dollar? The answer is not many—which is why systems based on finding foreclosure, pre-foreclosure, fixer-upper, and tax-sale properties are so difficult for the average investor.

In contrast, there are many more people than you might think who would be willing to sell you their property for ninety cents on the dollar. The key to successfully negotiating a $90,000 sales price for a $100,000 property lies in knowing how to profile and find the types of sellers who would be most likely to sell their property for a small discount. Your real estate agent can greatly assist you with this by setting up a series of filters through which to search the MLS for suitable properties.

The way to get a 10 percent discount on a property (and quite possibly more) is to find a *motivated seller*. A motivated seller has some particular reason why they have to either raise money or sell their property quickly. Because time is an important factor to the motivated seller, they are most often likely to be somewhat flexible on their price in order to get the deal done. The way to find a motivated seller is to look for clues indicating that a seller might be facing personal circumstances that would cause him or her to want to sell quickly.

One example might be a vacant property. A vacant property indicates that the seller lives elsewhere, which could mean that they are paying two mortgages at the same time. Perhaps it is an estate sale situation where the heirs have acquired the property from a relative and have no use for it. Maybe the sellers had a job transfer or career change that has forced them to either relocate or downsize. Whatever the reason, a vacant property is often a good sign that a seller might be motivated to sell quickly, and therefore be somewhat flexible on price.

Other reasons why sellers might be particularly motivated to sell could be a divorce or marriage, a new baby, an
illness in the family, or the kids going off to college. Perhaps the lender has taken a property back and wants to
get it off their books. There are many reasons why a seller
might be particularly motivated and it will be yours and
your agent's job to find them out.

Some reasons, such as the property being vacant, are
apparent before you ever visit the property. Other reasons
might not come to light until you actually visit the property
and begin to talk with the seller. Many times, all it takes is
a simple question on your part, "So, why are you selling?"

You can have your real estate agent set up an automatic search for properties that have certain keywords in
the remarks section of the MLS listings. Typical keywords
might include, "vacant", "motivated seller", "bank owned",
"corporate owned", "estate sale", "divorce sale", "foreclosure", "pre-foreclosure", "relocation", etc. Have your agent
set up a search for listings containing keywords that might
indicate a particularly motivated seller.

A frequently overlooked technique for finding motivated
sellers is to search for properties that have been on the
market for longer than the average market time for that
type of property in that area. For example, if three-bedroom
houses in an area typically sell in an average of 42 days,
do you think that the sellers of properties that have been
on the market for more than 42 days might be starting to
get anxious? Even better, do you think that the real estate
agents for those listings might be getting anxious too?

Nearly all sellers start out overly optimistic with visions
of dollar signs dancing in their heads. From my experience
in dealing with thousands of sellers over the years, I can

tell you that sellers are often stubborn about maintaining their list price, holding on to the erroneous belief that buyers will come anyway, rather than dropping the price to an appropriate level. By the time they realize their mistake and lower the price, it is often too late. The listing has become stale and buyers are not interested anymore.

This is often the best time to negotiate a good deal. The sellers have become disillusioned and their agents are often worried that all of their time and effort will have been wasted. This is a time when you will often find the seller's own agent aggressively advocating on your behalf that the seller accept your lower than market value offer. Believe it or not, this type of scenario plays itself out everyday in the real estate world. Ask your real estate agent to set up an automatic search filter that looks for properties that have been on the market for longer than the average market time for the areas where you are interested in investing.

Along these same lines, have your real estate agent set up a search for properties that meet all of your criteria but have expired off the market. An expired listing is one that was listed on the market but failed to sell. Since the owners of these properties obviously wanted to sell at one time, there is a good chance that they still do.

The reason why many of these properties were not re-listed is often because the owners have become fed up and disappointed, not because they no longer want to sell. These owners are often much more realistic and much more willing to entertain offers once their property has expired off of the market. This is a potential source of good deals that you should have your real estate agent investigate.

Once you have identified specific properties as potential investments, have your agent set up appointments to tour the properties. As you are going through the properties there are certain things to keep in mind.

First, remember that if you do decide to make an offer, as soon as it gets accepted you should hire a licensed inspector to go over the property with a fine-toothed comb. Your goal on the initial visit is to get a big-picture feel for the overall condition of the property's structure and mechanicals (heating/cooling, electrical and plumbing systems, and the appliances). Initially, do not worry too much about cosmetic factors such as the condition of the paint and carpeting. Do not worry about a broken light switch or a broken closet door; you can get nit-picky during the negotiation phase, if it gets that far. For now, your visit should probably last no more than 30 minutes, and more likely about twenty minutes.

Before you go inside the property, take a walk around the outside to look for obvious problems. Are the roof shingles straight or are they curled? Are the gutters in good condition and firmly attached? What about the windows—are the window frames in good shape and are the windowpanes themselves free of cracks and internal moisture build-up? Again, do not worry about such things as peeling paint or a broken doorknob, which are very easy to fix; pay attention to the overall condition of the big stuff.

Are the driveway and walkway cracked and crumbly, or are they in good shape? What about the garage—if it is a detached garage, what is the condition of its roof? Is the garage door operable? Is there a fence and is it in good shape, or does it need to be replaced—can it get by with only a paint job?

As you move on to the inside of the house, do not worry about whether the housekeeping is up to your standards.

Quite frankly, the worse the house looks on the inside the better it will be for you from a negotiating standpoint. Do not worry about wild paint schemes or poor taste in furnishings. You are looking for signs of a good basic structure. As you walk around the house look at all of the ceilings and around all of the window frames for signs of leaking and water damage. Turn on all of the faucets and check for good drainage and good water pressure (do the same for the shower/bathtub) and flush all of the toilets.

Turn on both the heat and (if applicable) the air-conditioning units and wait to see if the heat/air actually gets hot/cold. Ask the owner or listing agent the age of such things as the roof, water heater, furnace, air-conditioner, and appliances. Ask when was the last time the heating/air-conditioning system was serviced by a licensed technician. Ideally, newer is better than older, but brand-new is by no means necessary. For example, for a roof that typically lasts about fifteen years, it would be nice to have a roof that was newer than seven or eight years old, so that you could feel confident that the roof was not going to become an issue at any time in the near future.

When you go into the basement (if there is one), look around all of the baseboards and along the bottom foot or so of all of the walls for signs of water damage. Use your nose to sniff for a pronounced damp, musty smell in the basement, which might possibly be a sign of water seepage or flooding problems.

Again, you are not a property inspector; so do not get bogged down in the details. Your goal for the initial walk-thru is to get a feel for the overall structural integrity of the property and whether or not you would like to make an offer. If need be, you can always clean, paint, and change carpet, all of which are relatively cheap and easy to do. While you should certainly try to purchase properties that need as little fix-up as possible, you should never let poor cosmetics get in your way of a good deal.

Once you begin actively looking at properties there will invariably be those that you quickly rule out as potential investments and those that you decide are worth pursuing. For those that are worth pursuing, it is time to start making offers.

# Chapter 12

## Winning Negotiation Tactics

A well-worn saying within real estate investment circles is, "You don't make your money when you sell, you make it when you buy." While the *WealthLoop* system affords you several avenues for making money and maximizing your return on investments, there is some truth to this old saying. You have got to buy the right type of property, and in the right neighborhood, and in the right price range, in order to make the system work for you. In other words, you have to do the right things up front to maximize the amount of money you make on your deals.

We have already gone over the important aspects of locating and screening properties. You know enough to never make an offer on a property that does not meet your basic investment criteria and pass your initial walk-thru assessment. Having found the right property, it is time to negotiate the best deal.

Every seller has a number in their head below which they will not sell their property—their "go/no-go" price. This price is *always* below the asking price. Your job in any negotiation is to find the go/no-go price hidden in the seller's head. Every dollar that you pay above the go/no-go price is a dollar that you did not have to pay had you effectively done your negotiating homework.

Let's talk a minute about negotiating *attitude* and *etiquette*. Since I do not know another way to get the point across quite so succinctly, I am just going to put it out there— whenever you find yourself in a negotiation DON'T BE A HORSE'S ASS! Sorry about that, but it has to be said.

I cannot tell you how many times I have been in a negotiating situation where one of the parties took an obstinate and antagonistic stance towards the other party. It is as if they watched too many bad TV shows and thought that the way to get what they wanted was to play the role of a tough guy. WRONG!

The fact of the matter is that if you are likeable, generous in your appreciation of the other party's situation, and willing to work towards a win-win solution to any problem, you are MUCH more likely to eventually get the deal that YOU want. Be nice even if the other guy is not—two obstinate people do not make for a smoother negotiation!

People like doing business with people they like, and people do not like doing business with people they don't like. Be nice. Ask polite questions. Always seek a compromise solution that works for everyone. Never forget the golden rule of negotiating, "You will always get what you want if you can figure out a way to give the other person what they want." This applies both to your negotiations with property sellers when you are buying properties and your negotiations with tenant/buyers when you are selling properties.

Another thing to keep in mind is that you should never come off as a big-shot investor. If you try to act like you know everything there is to know about real estate you may end up both intimidating and insulting the seller at the same time, which immediately starts you off on the wrong foot.

Remember that you want the seller to like you and to want to make a deal with you. No matter how experienced you might become, always maintain a low-key approach. NEVER argue with a seller, *even if you know that something they are saying is wrong—just let it pass.* Enough said about attitude and etiquette.

So, your mission in any negotiation, either in person or through your agent, is to learn as much about the seller's personal situation and motivations as possible. Before actually entering into negotiations you can check such things as the county tax records to see if tax payments are up to date, and the zoning and compliance records to see if any code violations have been recorded against the property. These are things that you can have your real estate agent do for you. And if anything negative comes up you can use them as bargaining chips later on. In many areas of the country these types of searches can now be done quickly online, so doing them is not as big a deal as it might sound.

As your agent is contacting the listing agents or sellers to set up the initial appointments to see properties, she should be casually asking questions regarding the sellers' situation. Try to have her schedule your showings for times that you think the sellers will be home, so you can ask questions directly of the seller. Good questions to ask include:

- How long have you lived here?

- What problems have you had with the house?
- Why are you moving?
- Are you staying in town, or are you moving out of town?
- When do you have to report to your new job?
- Have you already found a place to stay when you sell?
- Are the kids already registered in their new school?
- How quickly would you want to close? Why so quick/long?
- How long has the property been on the market?
- How many offers have you had?
- Why didn't you accept any of the offers?
- Do you know of any outstanding violations on the property?
- What things would I have to fix if I bought the property?
- How much would you be willing to take for your property?

Of course, if you come off sounding like a prosecuting attorney your questions will be met with suspicion. Ask your questions using a friendly, conversational tone. Your questions should come up as a natural part of the small talk that develops between you and the seller. Be genuine in your desire to get to know the seller and his situation and do not sound like you are rattling off a memorized list.

Another thing to keep in mind as you are negotiating a transaction is to never let yourself become emotionally attached to a particular property. A house is an asset—it is a thing. If the neighborhood, property type and condition, and numbers are not right, walk away from the deal and go find another one. Never let yourself get blinded by the pretty garden or the gorgeous fireplace to the extent that you lose objectivity and end up purchasing a property that is not right for your wealth building plan.

Treat properties as a business, and nothing more. Neither you, nor your agent should be making too many calls to the seller during the negotiation process because it makes you appear too eager. If the seller calls you, and if you are interested in the property, you should play it safe by calmly saying something like, "The property seemed okay but the price was a little high for what I'm looking for." Let the seller make the next move. Let him come to you. Maintain an attitude of matter-of-fact neutrality and never show your enthusiasm for a property in front of the seller.

Just as important, NEVER be rude by trash talking a property in front of the seller. Do not be afraid to point out obvious flaws in the property, but do so in a diplomatic way that does not offend the seller. You can use these flaws as bargaining chips later on. You want the seller to know that you know that the property is less than perfect.

Use the information that you gather to set your offer up with built-in bargaining chips that you can bargain away as needed. For example, if you find out that the seller would like to move on April 1st, you might write your offer with a May 1st closing date. You could then offer a closing date concession to the seller in exchange for a concession on his part.

In any negotiation it is in your best interest to make any flaws in the property appear more important to you than they really are. Do not be ridiculous about it, but appropriately playing up flaws serves two purposes: 1) it leaves the door open for you to ask for price concessions and/or repair credits, and 2) it gives you something to give back to the seller to make him/her feel like they are not having to make all of the concessions in the negotiation.

This last point deserves some comment. Let's say that during the course of the negotiations you ask the seller for five particular concessions. Little does the seller know that you are truly concerned about only one of these concessions, but have included the other four to use as bargaining chips. Now, as you work to strike a bargain, you have four concessions that YOU can make to the seller. You might end up giving back all four items, or just one or two, but by having built these bargaining chips into your initial offer you allow the seller to feel that he/she was not out-negotiated by you.

Be careful of sellers who try to turn the tables on you. If you find that a seller or their agent is asking YOU a lot of questions, recognize that they are trying to determine YOUR personal situation and motivation so THEY can get the best price for themselves! If you pick up on a seller trying to feel you out, remain cool and detached in your responses.

If they ask you if you like their property, say, "I'm not sure. I wanted to compare it to another I'm considering." If they ask you about the other property you are considering say, "It's not too far from here and it's priced lower." If they ask you what your price range is say, "Your price is a little bit higher than I am planning on spending; how much would you be willing to take?"

No matter what you do, do not be specific in your answers and never be the first to mention an actual price. The one who mentions a number first loses! You want to figure out the seller's bottom line but you do not want him to figure out yours. Saying, "I'm not sure," or "I'll have to think about it," are always good ways to avoid answering a specific question.

In all of your negotiations, remember that in order for you to get what you want you have to give the seller what he wants. If the seller feels that you are getting the better end of the bargain he will not want to do a deal with you, but if he feels that you are giving up as much as he is, he will be much more likely to make concessions. Build plausible bargaining chips into your offers, so that you leave room for the seller to haggle with you. Be careful about crossing the line between pointing out flaws for negotiation purposes and inadvertently insulting the seller. And while you never want to argue with the seller, you have to keep your objectivity and be prepared to walk away from a deal if you cannot make it work.

Lest you believe that all negotiations take place before a formal written offer is presented, understand that in reality the negotiation process is a timeline that plays itself out from the moment you meet a seller until the moment a final contract is signed. The period before submitting a written offer typically centers on the parties feeling each other out and gathering information. Hard-core price negotiations usually do not take place until after a formal written offer is submitted.

The most important thing to remember is that as long as you enter into every negotiation with a clear set of objectives with respect to the type, condition, and price of property that you are looking for, it will be virtually impossible for you to not make profits of several hundred percent on each of your properties!

# Chapter 13

## The Right Way to Present Offers

There are a thousand creative ways to protect yourself when writing offers and here are a few you can use as needed:

1.   When entering your name on a written offer/contract, instead of writing "John Q. Smith," add the following tagline afterwards, "and/or assigns." By writing your name as "John Q. Smith, and/or assigns," this gives you the right to assign the contract to another party if necessary.

2.   Always make sure that your agent includes a clause in the offer allowing for an inspection period of five to ten days, which allows you to get out of the deal if you do not approve of the inspection results. ALWAYS use the inspection period to hire a professional home inspector to make sure that everything is in good working order. Better to pay a couple of hundred bucks and find out that you do not really want the property than to be stuck with a lemon.

3.   Always write your offer "contingent upon financing." This will allow you to get out of the deal if your financing falls through for some reason.

4. Explain to the sellers that you are an investor and will ultimately be renting the property to tenants. Try to get them to accept a contract contingency that allows you to show the property to prospective tenants even before you actually close on the property and ownership transfers. In most instances this will allow you to get the property rented even before you actually own it (when renting to a tenant/buyer in this situation, make sure that you have a contingency written into your agreement with the tenant/buyer stating that your lease with them is contingent upon you actually receiving title to the property).

5. If you are not 100 percent sure about a property but you want to lock it up for a few days to think about it or get a second opinion, you can always have your agent insert a clause into the contract that makes your offer contingent upon your partner's approval. Your partner can be whoever you want them to be in this situation, and if they do not approve of the property you can easily back out of the deal without penalty.

6. In some states, attorneys get involved in closings and in other states title companies handle the closings without the parties hiring attorneys. If you're in a state where attorneys handle closings, insert a five- to ten-day "attorney review clause" into your offer/contract, so you can back out of the deal without penalty should your attorney not approve (NOTE: The attorney review period is NOT used as an opportunity to renegotiate price! The attorney review is related strictly to the legality of the documents and the transaction terms, clauses, dates, etc.).

7. Always purchase a buyer's title insurance policy and

always request that the seller purchase a seller's title insurance policy. By ensuring that all parties to the transaction have purchased title insurance you can be certain that the title to the property you are purchasing is "clean." And if any title problems arise in the future, you will be compensated for any damages that might result.

8. Finally, try to arrange for either yourself or your agent to be present when your offer is given to the seller. This will allow you to judge their reaction and come up with a strategy for responding to any objections. It also puts a human face on things and can help avoid any unintended misunderstandings. Remember that you never want to insult or agitate a seller, even unintentionally. In many parts of the country this simply is not the way things are done. The buyer's agent faxes offers to the seller's agent, who presents the offer to their seller. But if you can possibly be there, by all means try to be.

# Chapter 14

## The Key to Attracting Hordes of Quality Tenant/Buyers

It is helpful to think of the *WealthLoop* system as having two distinct phases: the property phase and the people phase. The property phase is about location, features, condition and price. The people phase is about finding a good tenant/buyer for your property and negotiating a rent-to-own deal with them.

Finding a good tenant/buyer is like finding a big fat sparkling nugget of pure gold! Each tenant/buyer that enters into a rent-to-own agreement with you represents a several hundred percent return on your investment, and propels you that much closer to your goal of creating financial independence for yourself and your family. As every gold prospector knows, the only way to find the nuggets is to "sift through the sand," which is what you will have to do with respect to finding good tenant/buyers.

By sifting through the sand I mean that you are going to have to make your phone ring. You are going to have to get prospective tenant/buyers to call you. The more calls you can generate, the more opportunities you will have to select the very best tenant/buyers for your properties. Like anything else in life, the way to get what you want (lots of calls) is to give the other people what they want: an offer/ opportunity that is too good to pass up.

Remember that your tenant/buyer prospects are people that want to own their own home, but for whom the possibility of doing such seems closed to them. Since they do not even think that it is in the realm of possibility for them to buy a home of their own, many are not even looking to do so. *And therein lies your opportunity.* The *WealthLoop* system incorporates an autopilot prospecting program that can generate all of the tenant/buyer calls you will ever need!

Imagine yourself in the shoes of one of your prospective tenant/buyers, and as you are scanning through the local newspaper in search of a place to rent you come across the following ads:

*Note: These are real ads. Only the phone numbers have been changed.*

---

**Clark and Peterson**
area. Three blocks west from
Clark/Ridge, house, 3 bedrooms,
central heat. Will help with winter
heating. $1200 heat included.
111-222-3333

---

**Jumbo Rent-to-Own!**
Spacious home on peaceful,
tree-lined street features sunny and
open family-sized eat-in kitchen,
gleaming hardwood floors,
large yard w/shade-trees,
full finished basement.
**Credit problems okay!**
**Free Recorded Message.**
**Call**
**1-800-111-2222 ID#1234**

---

**West Lincoln Park.**
3 bedroom has sunny rooms,
hardwood floors,
modern kitchen and central ac.
222-333-4444

---

So, which ad would you *have to* call? If you were only allowed to call one of the ads, which one would it be? Well, if you are like 99.9 percent of the people on the planet it would have to be the middle ad!

The middle ad accomplishes three important things:

1.  It paints a beautiful "mind picture" of a big space in a nice neighborhood that you are compelled to want to know more about.
2.  Offers the possibility of ownership in spite of credit problems.
3.  Offers a non-threatening, recorded message that allows you to get information without the pressure or embarrassment of having to talk to a live person.

Notice how the ad uses *descriptive language* designed to evoke a positive emotional response from the reader. These words evoke an overall picture of the property and the offer, rather than coming off as a list of items. Take another look at all of the descriptive language used in the ad: *jumbo, rent-to-own, spacious, peaceful, tree-lined, sunny and open, family-sized, gleaming, shade trees, credit problems okay, free recorded message.* I want you to promise you will NEVER write an ad like this: (This is a real ad)

**Rosemont Township.**
Three bedroom, two bath,
close to the bus line.
Newer water heater and
tile in kitchen. $1300.
111-222-3333

You should be talking about the, "Fantastic and spacious home, in excellent condition, with a lovely view of the park, and easy rent-to-own terms," and not the number of bedrooms, large water heater, or newer toilet! Also, ALWAYS place your ad in the Houses For Rent section of the classifieds and NEVER in the Houses For Sale section.

A descriptive ad will make the phone ring off the hook and the overall system is very easy to implement. There are numerous companies that offer personal 800 phone numbers with voicemail and unlimited ID# mailboxes for as little as $10 a month and about ten cents per call. Some systems even have fax-back features that allow callers to request such things as floor plans and a map of the neighborhood that have been stored in the system and made available to callers.

These systems allow you to filter out the curious from the serious, because only those who are still interested and meet the basic qualifications that you have set out in the recording will bother to leave a voicemail with their contact information. The system operates 24 hours a day, seven days a week, and frees you from being tied to a telephone. You only have to deal with those people that have passed your initial screening and are serious enough to have left their contact information. At the end of the book you will find a sample voicemail script that has proven effective.

The same principle that holds true for your ads holds true for your signs. While you certainly have less space to work with on a sign than in an ad, you still want to make a powerful statement that compels prospective tenant/buyers to call. Rather than a sign with the words "For Rent" and your phone number, you can get a 2' x 3' (big is good) corrugated plastic sign custom made for about $40. Here's an example of an effective sign:

HOUSE
FOR SALE
Seller-Financing

24-hr Recorded Info:
1-800-123-4567
ID#1230

RENT – TO – OWN
Credit Problems Okay

# Chapter 15

## The Right Way to Show Tenant/Buyers Your Properties

It is important that all of your showings are orchestrated and timed to proceed exactly the way that YOU want. You only give the information that you want to give, when you want to give it. Do not give up control of the showings just because someone asks you to. Stay focused and you will get rich!

First and foremost, DO NOT set individual showings! This is one area where your "800" number can be of great help. When people call to listen to your recorded information all they will hear is a description of the property, the property address, the fact that all applicants will undergo formal credit and background checks, and the date and time for the Open House they can attend if they want to see the property.

It is important that you DO NOT talk about prices, rent amounts, terms, qualifications, or anything else having anything to do with the rent-to-own program before they visit the property and submit an application. At this point you only want them to decide whether to come and see the property, or not. Here is a sample script for your "800" number recording:

> *Hello and thank you for calling on this beautiful rent-to-own property located at 1234 Main St. in Happy Valley. The house is in great condition and sits on a corner lot with a large fenced yard with beautiful shade trees. Inside you'll find three good sized, carpeted bedrooms, 1 ½ updated baths, a large living room/family room with gleaming wood floors, eat-in-kitchen with brand new appliances, including dishwasher and built-in microwave, full finished basement, and an attached garage. Oops! Almost forgot to mention the central heat and air! One look at this beautiful house and you'll want to move right in! We are having an open house on Saturday morning between 11:00 am and 11:45 am, and another on Tuesday evening from 6:00 pm to 6:45 pm. Feel free to come on by, and if you like it be prepared to fill out an application. We are offering easy owner financing/rent-to-own terms so don't be shy if your credit is less than perfect – it's okay. Just the same, we do require a complete credit and background check of all applicants. Thanks for calling!*

The rent-to-own program takes some time to explain and is difficult to do except one-on-one and on paper. You do not want to waste your time explaining the program to everyone that asks. Wait until they have already seen the property and you know that they like it. Also, never explain the program over the phone because you run a very high risk of confusing them and turning them off to a program that might really be just what they are looking for.

You benefit in two ways by using the Open House approach to showings. By showing many people at once you save a lot of time and you create an auction-like atmosphere that generates excitement and competition amongst the prospective tenant/buyers. Nothing gets a person as motivated as the prospect of having something they want pulled out from under them by a competitor.

Try to limit the time frame for your open houses. I would say that you should never go longer than an hour and a half—forty-five minutes is ideal. You want the open house to look busy to the people that show up. Schedule open houses at various times, so that you can accommodate people on different schedules. You might offer a Saturday morning open house from 11:00 – 11:45 and a Tuesday evening open house from 6:30 –7:15. You can experiment with the days, times, and lengths of time to see what works best for you and your area.

If you absolutely must set an individual showing due to a prospective tenant/buyer's unusual schedule, do so only after you have confirmed that they have already driven by the property and like the house and the neighborhood.

On the day of your open house you want the property to shine inside and out! Manicured lawn, clean interior, ALL of the lights on, a radio with soft music lowly playing in the background, temperature set for comfort, the scent of air-freshener throughout. You want the property to make a great first impression. You want the prospective tenant/buyers that stop by to be impressed with the property and to visualize themselves living there.

Once people start to arrive it is important that you have

every one of them sign in—no exceptions! Name, address, phone number, and e-mail address is good. Also, have a space where they can indicate how they found out about the property and the open house (this will indicate the effectiveness of your various advertising methods). Tell them they are free to walk through the property and that you will be happy to answer any questions *after* they have walked through. Do not follow them, and do not give them a tour. Let them go on their merry way. If they are interested they will come back to talk to you and if they are not they will leave when they are through. You only want to spend your time with people who have walked through the property, who like what they see, and who express a definite interest.

Once they have walked through the property on their own, and if they have expressed an interest, you can explain how the rent-to-own program works. First give a general explanation, and if they understand and are receptive, use a worksheet to go over the program on paper (you can find a blank copy of the worksheet at the end of the book).

When going over the program on paper, give them three alternatives to consider. These alternatives are based on different rental amounts and different up-front money amounts. The following example shows what the worksheet might look like for a three-year rent-to-own program that assumes a current market value of $110,000, annual appreciation of 4%, and where the tenant says they can pay $4,500 up front.

Walk each prospective tenant through their own worksheet based on their own numbers. Explain how the numbers work in their favor the more rent they pay (bigger credits) and the more money they put up-front (less to finance when they exercise their option). Of course, you should know what your break-even rent is long before you ever get in front of a prospective tenant. Practice going through the worksheet on your own; this is your prime selling tool and you do not want to mess up your presentation and lose a good prospective tenant/buyer.

| | Option 1 | Option 2 | Option 3 |
|---|---|---|---|
| Monthly Rent: | $ 1,200 | $ 1,350 | $ 1500 |
| Monthly Rent Credit: | $ 100 | $ 300 | $ 500 |
| Annual Rent Credit: | $ 1,200 | $ 3,600 | $ 6,000 |
| 36 Month Purchase Price: | $124,000 | $124,000 | $124,000 |
| 36 Month Rent Credit: | <$3,600> | <$10,800> | <$18,000> |
| Up-front Payment: | <$4,500> | <$4,500> | <$4,500> |
| Final Tenant Balance: | $115,900 | $108,700 | $101,500 |

**Here's Why Renting-to-Own Makes Sense:**
1. **Build Equity Fast:** With a conventional mortgage, only a few dollars a month goes towards equity – most of your payments go towards interest. Renting-to-own builds equity faster!
2. **Avoid Bank Hassles:** Unless you have good credit to start with, renting-to-own may be your only realistic opportunity to own your own home in the near future.
3. **Build Credit:** By living up to your agreement and paying your rent on time, you build a strong, positive credit history that can benefit you on into the future.
4. **Flexible Options:** Unlike bank financing, renting-to-own gives you the option of purchasing the property without the obligation!

Structure the options so that each higher rent amount leads to a proportionately higher rental credit to the tenant/buyer. In the above example, Option 2 rent is $150 higher per month but the rent credit is $200 a month higher. Rent Option 3 is another $150 per month higher but the rent credit is again $200 a month higher. This gives the prospective tenant/buyer a strong incentive to go for either options #2 or #3. As for you, you are only giving up a few dollars worth of extra credit in exchange for much more positive cash flow now.

By the way, you are not offering them the option to make one of the three different rent payments each month! They must pick one of the options up front and stick with it throughout the term of the lease agreement. If you allow them to make flexible monthly rental payments you are getting yourself into a bookkeeping nightmare!

Once you have gone through the worksheet with a prospective tenant/buyer, and if they are still interested, ask them to fill out a rental application. It is important that you DO NOT give them an application to take away. Again, DO NOT give them an application to take away.

Explain that you have several interested parties and will be making your decision in a few days. Let them know that if they are serious they are more than welcome to take five minutes to fill out the application on the spot. Also, and this is VERY important, let them know that you will be paying to do a reference check as part of the process, so there is a $35 fee if they want to complete the application.

You might be wondering why I am so adamant about insisting that you DO NOT let them take the application with them, and that you DO NOT let them fill out the application without first receiving the $35 application fee. The reason for being adamant is that this is a very important filter that enables you to weed out all but the most serious candidates; you actually want people to balk at having to complete the application on the spot and having to pay a $35 application fee. How serious can somebody be if they are reluctant, or unable, to scrape up a mere $35 in exchange for the opportunity to own a beautiful home of their own?

Believe it or not, many people take the step of asking potential tenant/buyers for a rental application, but neglect to actually follow through by checking their references. I want you to promise yourself to always call every reference listed. You will be amazed by what people will tell you about a person if you simply ask. By checking with past and current employers, landlords, and credit references you can save yourself a lot of headaches and heartache, so do not skimp on this very important step.

Save yourself a lot of aggravation and approach the application process as a test that the applicant must pass before you will take them seriously. Always make a prospective tenant/buyer feel like you have a stack of completed applications. If they think they are the only ones interested in the property you will be in a much weaker negotiating position than if they think that they are competing against other qualified and interested applicants.

Once they have completed the application and handed it to you, politely ask them for their driver's license to verify their personal information. Tell them that you will be calling them within a couple of days. Explain that one of the factors for approving an applicant is the amount of money they are able to put down on the property. Ask them how much they would be able to put down.

It is important that you DO NOT give them an amount, but that they give you an amount. If they ask you how much you require, explain to them that there really is no set amount. Let them know how serious you are about finding an applicant who is very committed to purchasing the property at the end of the lease period, and that it has been your experience that the applicant who is able to put down the most money is usually the most serious. Remind them that all of the down payment is fully credited towards the purchase price unless they back out of the deal and do not purchase the property.

After explaining your position, ask them again how much they are able to put down. No matter what they say, ask them if they could come up with just a little bit more. Not at the initial meeting, but on a subsequent follow-up call, you might want to let them know that you feel they are the best applicant, but that there is another good applicant who is able to put down more money. Again, ask them what is the most money they can put down. If necessary, offer to accept a higher rent payment for the first few months in order to give them the opportunity to come up with the additional funds.

Once you have decided to accept a particular applicant, set an appointment as soon as possible to sign the paperwork (an example rent-to-own agreement can be found at the back of the book). Remind them to bring a money order or cashier's check (not a personal check) for the up-front payment amount and first month's rent. Go over the program one last time, make sure they are committed, explain your rules and make sure they understand them, and have them sign the agreement.

Be wary of getting so excited about having found what you believe to be a good tenant/buyer that you make foolish and costly mistakes. Remain businesslike in your interactions with prospective tenant/buyers. Never, never, never agree to rent to someone because you feel sorry for them.

I would also suggest that you never agree to a rent-to-own arrangement with family, or friends. If they fail to go through with the deal you will feel obligated (and they will make you feel obligated) to give them their money back. If you remain honest and true to the agreement they will hate you forever. If you go back on your word by breaking the agreement and giving them "your" money back you will have completely wasted several years worth of profits.

Never give a tenant/buyer the keys until the up-front payment and first month's rent have cleared the bank. If they ask if they can start to move things in early you must be firm and say no. You must *train your tenant/buyers* right from the start that you will do everything by the book. Do not ever deviate from the agreement. Doing such would be like sticking a sharp stick in your eye. By deviating from the exact letter of your agreement you will be opening yourself up to untold heartache and sorrow. Be firm. This is a business.

I also recommend that for your peace of mind you never give tenant/buyers your home address or home phone number. Think about it, do you have your doctor's home number and address? What about your accountant's? What about your attorney's? If you act like a professional business person you will be treated like a professional business person. Professional business people have business addresses and phones – they don't work out of their houses, so neither should you appear to.

Spend a couple of bucks a month on a P.O. Box that you will use as your exclusive business address and get a dedicated cell phone or land-line that you use only for business (both of these items are tax deductible expenses). You might also consider un-listing your home phone number from the telephone directory.

Finally, being firm, businesslike, and strictly by the book is not the same thing as taking advantage of people.

Remember that what holds true when negotiating with sellers also holds true when negotiating with tenant buyers: *nobody is going to want to do a deal with you if they feel that they are getting the short end of the stick.* Be fair, honest and straightforward with all of your tenant/buyers and you have a 99 percent chance that they will act the same towards you. Set the rules up front and stick to them. Your tenant/buyers do not have to like you but they do have to respect you.

# Chapter 16

## Creating Your Own Million-Dollar WealthLoop

At this point you know a lot more than you think you do. You have a clear understanding of:

- The basic economics of putting together a rent-to-own deal using the *WealthLoop* system;
- Things to look for when analyzing markets for potential communities and neighborhoods to invest in;
- The type of properties and price range to concentrate on;
- The basic things to look for on an initial visit to a property;
- The attitude and mindset of a successful negotiator;
- How to show your properties to potential tenant/buyers.

While you might still feel that there are a million things that you have to know, the truth is that you now know enough to get started on the road to personal wealth creation. Believe it or not, you now have all of the tools you will need to set your own course towards financial freedom. What is important now is that you chart your course and begin moving forward. It is time for you to formulate your personal action plan.

The very first thing that I want you to do is to buy a house. I want you to buy it within 30 days, which is double the time you really need. I doubled the time, because I assume that you are scared witless and will need two weeks to talk yourself into starting!

Seriously though, it should take you no more than seven to ten days to zero-in on good neighborhoods within an hour of your home that have nice three-bedroom, one and one-half bath houses, and if applicable in your part of the country, basements and garages.

Concurrently with your neighborhood research, take the first seven to ten days to contact several real estate agents and mortgage brokers. (Hint: real estate agents are excellent resources for finding good mortgage brokers, inspectors, and anyone else you will need.) Do not randomly call real estate agents. Call the agents who have a market presence in the neighborhoods you are interested in. (Hint: I would be wary of working with an agent that has been in the real estate business for less than two years, who works the business part-time, or who sells less than one property a month.)

Unless you have a well-established relationship with a particular bank, I would stick with mortgage brokers and avoid banks. Banks have one source of funds—their own. Mortgage brokers, on the other hand, are middlemen that bring borrowers and lenders together and a good mortgage broker might have 40 or 50 sources of funds, which means they will be able to fit you to the best rates and best programs available for what you are trying to accomplish.

As in any profession, there are good mortgage brokers and bad mortgage brokers, so try to get a recommendation from someone that has actually worked with a particular mortgage broker and has found them to be honest and hard-working (Again, a good real estate agent should be able to provide a recommendation or two).

Make sure that both your real estate agent and mortgage broker know exactly what you want to accomplish and how you plan to go about it. Give them each a copy of this book to make sure they understand exactly what it is that you are trying to do. Do not work with any real estate agent or mortgage broker who seems to not "get it" or who acts like what you are trying to do is too difficult or even impossible. Just keep sifting through agents and brokers until you find a couple of them who understand and approve of your plan. You cannot afford to have anyone on your team that is less than 100 percent committed to your success!

Understand that as an investor you will likely be paying slightly higher interest rates and fees on your loans. That is just the way it is for investors, so get used to it. That said, the interest rate you pay really does not matter so long as the payment is equal to or lower than the income you will be generating. Forget about rates and think in terms of total income versus total costs. As long as your income covers your costs, you are safe.

When discussing your plans with mortgage brokers I want you to ask about "80/15/5" investor loan programs. What this means is that they are giving you a first loan for 80 percent of the sale price, a second loan for 15 percent of the sale price, with the remaining five percent coming from you as a down payment. This type of loan will allow you to avoid paying PMI and should lower the overall cost of your loan.

I want you to ask if they have "interest-only" loans for investors. If they do, you might want to look at the numbers to see if this type of loan makes sense for any particular deal. An interest-only loan means that you are not paying anything towards principle payoff with each monthly payment. While I would never recommend an interest-only loan for your personal residence, this can be a very useful tool for the purchase of investment properties.

It is natural if you are feeling a little intimidated by the prospect of actually getting started, but you *must* get into *action* immediately. You know enough to review the numbers to see if any particular deal makes sense. You are smart enough to subtract the costs from the rents to see if it is a positive or negative number. If it is a positive number you do the deal and if it is a negative number you do not do the deal. This is not rocket science.

Part of the reason for finding a good real estate agent and mortgage broker who understands what it is that you are trying to accomplish is that they will be there to help you analyze each and every deal before you do it. You do not have to worry because you will not be alone. Their success will be tied to your success, which is why you want to assemble a good team from the start.

Okay, in the first seven to ten days you will be scouting neighborhoods and speaking with real estate agents and mortgage brokers. By the end of the second week you will have your initial team in place and you will be ready to begin looking at properties. Also by the end of the first two weeks you should have made a formal loan application with your chosen lender so that you will be ready to go once you select a property to purchase.

Weeks two and three should be devoted to looking at properties. You should be able to find a property to make an offer on within the first five to ten properties you see. If you do not make an offer after seeing ten properties you are doing something wrong. Either you have selected the wrong neighborhood or you have the fool idea in your head that you have to look at 600 properties before making an offer, which is utter nonsense and an excuse for inaction.

Once you find a nice property in a nice neighborhood in the right price range, BUY IT! It does not matter if it was the first property you looked at or the tenth. A nice property is a nice property and looking at more properties is not going to make it any better or any worse.

By the end of thirty days you should have made one or more offers and purchased an investment property. As soon as you have an accepted offer you should order a "Rent-To-Own" sign and a personal 800 phone number. If you have received permission from the seller of the property you just purchased, you can start running classified ads and setting open houses immediately. If you do exactly as you have learned, the chances are good that you can have a deal with a good tenant/buyer even before you close on the property. Of course, you will have written your tenant/buyer deal to be contingent upon you actually closing on the property.

Once you have purchased your first property and have a good tenant/buyer in place I want you to IMMEDIATELY GO OUT AND DO IT AGAIN! You should own two investment properties and have them rented out to good tenant/buyers within 90 days of starting the program. Once you have two properties under your belt you can take a step back to reevaluate.

Why do I recommend that you go out and buy your first property within 30 days and have two properties within 90 days? I do it because the experience will liberate your mind from the psychological chains that have thus far bound you to financial mediocrity. By going through the experience in such a whirlwind fashion you will gain a sense of confidence that you have never before experienced. You will fully and completely, deep into the core of your very soul, understand that you really can become rich and that this really is a simple and nearly foolproof path to personal wealth creation.

Once you have achieved this, a true inner knowledge that you can make this work, you will be unstoppable! You will be able to do it again, and again, and again! You will be able to continue buying investment properties and when your tenant/buyers eventually buy your properties you will take the proceeds to buy even more properties using 1031 Exchanges to defer taxes and increase your wealth even more. You will have received the greatest gift a person can receive: the gift of faith, self-confidence, and the motivation to succeed. You will have created your *WealthLoop.*

# Chapter 17

## Behold Your Future

Your journey of self-discovery and self-mastery has begun. Your decision to pursue a personal *WealthLoop* is firm, and you are committed to achieving your goal of financial freedom. You know that you have a proven system upon which to rely, so even when temporary setbacks show themselves, you pledge to learn from them and to continue onward until you achieve your goal. At this stage of the game it is crucial that you maintain a clear image of your desired outcome.

Imagine that you are looking backwards from six years in the future and you have achieved your goal—you are financially free! As you recall that first property you bought six years earlier, a smile passes over your face and you marvel at how far you have come, not only in terms of your finances, but also with respect to your knowledge, ability, and self-confidence. When you started out you were timid and naïve, but now you are a sophisticated, financially successful investor. My, how things have changed!

Back when you purchased that first property, the thought of putting out $5,000 scared the daylights out of you, but now you deal regularly in amounts ten times more than that with ease and confidence. In the beginning you had so many fears: "What if I can't find tenants?" "What if they don't buy the property at the end of the lease?" "What if I make a mistake?" By the time you bought your second property you were feeling a little more confident, but you still had a long way to go.

Still and all, and in spite of all of your fear and worrying, you ended your first year as an investor using the *Wealth-Loop* system having purchased three properties. You began to realize that all of your fears were basically unfounded. You found that it was really not all that difficult to find good tenant/buyers, and your doubts about whether the system would actually work faded as you found that most of the prospective tenant/buyers that you spoke with were actually very excited by the prospect of being able to pur-chase a home of their own. You found that rather than having to scramble to find tenant/buyers, your problem was trying to figure out which one of the applicants to ulti-mately select!

During that first year you managed to purchase your first two properties with the money you were able to scrape together yourself, and the third was purchased with the up-front money you received from the first three tenant/buyers who leased your houses. By the end of the first year and the beginning of the second year you were on fire! You were excited! You could see that it was working for you!

By the beginning of the second year you owned three properties and had several hundred dollars of positive cash flow coming in every month. You were hooked on investing using the *WealthLoop* system. Rather than wast-ing your newfound income on toys, you decided to do the smart thing and feed your money-machines so that you could grow your income even faster.

You took all of your positive cash flow and added some more of your own money that you had managed to save and bought two additional houses that second year. By the end of the second year you owned FIVE properties! Better still, as you moved into the third year the options from your first two properties came due and you were cashed out as they bought the properties according to the terms of your agreements with them.

Suddenly you found yourself sitting on a small pile of cash! Again, you did the right thing and plowed that money back into properties. By the end of the third year you had turned the first three properties into FOUR MORE properties! You used the up-front monies you received from your tenant/buyers to purchase a fifth property, and adding in the properties you purchased during the second year, you ended the third year of your investing career using the *WealthLoop* system with EIGHT properties!

Now you had some serious cash flow coming in every month and being a smart investor you continued to pour it into growing your *WealthLoop* and feeding your money-machines. You bought three more properties on your own with the cash flow and up-front monies you were receiving, plus the lease options on the three properties you bought during the second year came due, so you turned the profits from their sale into another six properties. Totaling it up, by the end of the fourth year you had FOURTEEN properties.

So here you are now, at the end of the fifth and beginning of the sixth year of your investing career. What with the lease options that came due at the end of the fifth year and because you continued to plow the money back into your investments, you now have over TWENTY properties! You have about half a million dollars in equity and positive cash flow of several thousand dollars a month! You have arrived!

|  | **Yr 1** | **Yr 2** | **Yr 3** | **Yr 4** | **Yr 5** |
|---|---|---|---|---|---|
| Bought | 2 | 3 | 5 | 9 | 13 |
| Sold | 0 | 0 | <2> | <3> | <5> |
| Had | 0 | 2 | 5 | 8 | 14 |
| Total | 2 | 5 | 8 | 14 | 22 |

This could be your reality. This will be your reality if you decide to make it so. It is easier than you might think it is right now, but if you commit and stay focused, you can do it! You have got to believe!

# Chapter 18

## Your Attitude Determines Your Future

The truth is that you can have whatever you want in life, as long as you have enough investments to pay for it. I have demonstrated how easy it is to acquire investment properties using the *WealthLoop*™ system. If you have any doubts or if you are hesitant in any way, you are sentencing yourself (and your family) to a life of financial mediocrity.

Whatever problems (I call these excuses) you might see with the system, recognize that the problems are within your mind and not within the system itself. The system is proven to work, however it is up to you to work the system. You must take ACTION! You must throw caution to the wind and proceed as if your financial future depended on it—damn the torpedoes, full speed ahead!

Rid yourself of the crazy notion that you have to know *everything* about something before acting on it. You only have to know *enough*, you do not have to know everything there is to know. After reading this book, *you know more than enough to make yourself rich*! Believe this, because it is the truth.

Do not listen to the people who will invariably begin telling you that your plans will never work—run from them! Stay focused and believe in yourself. If you suffer a setback, so what? Just pick yourself up, dust yourself off, and get right back at it. Making mistakes is part of the learning process. When you make mistakes you must learn from them and move on.

Believe that you will succeed. Believe that you will achieve financial freedom. Believe that you are just as good as any other person who has ever walked the earth and that you and your family deserve the best that life has to offer. Believe that you must take action immediately, before your desire and enthusiasm turns cold. Believe in yourself and go buy a house within the next thirty days and another within the next ninety days. Now go! The future is yours, and your attitude determines your future.

# Chapter 19

## Putting My Money Where My Mouth Is – A Case Study

This book is meant to motivate, empower, and instruct. While I hope that you find it entertaining, if an entertaining book is all that comes of my efforts I will have failed. I want you to actually go out and *act* on the information herein. I want you to take your first steps on the path to complete and everlasting financial freedom.

As I worked on the manuscript it became clear to me that I would have to *walk my talk* by doing myself that which I was asking you to do. While it is true that I have had many years of experience buying and selling houses, as I explained to you in the introduction to this book, for the past several years I had concentrated my business on multi-unit buildings and commercial properties. With my credibility on the line, I went out and bought a house.

This is probably the only house that was ever purchased just to prove a point, and I hope that my doing so proves to you that the principles you are learning are more than just the philosophical meanderings of a guy who likes to write—these principles really work in the real world. What follows is a textbook example of how simple and easy it is to make a profit buying nice single family houses in nice neighborhoods using the *WealthLoop* approach to real estate investing.

To keep things simple, I've rounded numbers (e.g.: I might say I received $3,000 when in fact it was only $2,854.60). My intention is to keep things simple, not to deceive. Please look past any inconsistencies to the bigger picture.

## Case Study: 123 Green St. (address changed to protect tenant's privacy)

I want you to meet a little *money-machine*. It's in Rockford, IL, which is about an hour's drive northwest of Chicago. Rockford is a nice little town with a population of about 152,000 people, having an average annual household income of about $52,000 in 2006. It is a typical Midwestern working-class community if there ever was one.

Nothing fancy about Rockford, but it is a nice town. It has a good feeling to it. While a studio apartment in Chicago could easily cost $150,000 or more, in Rockford you can buy a very nice single family house with a yard, basement, garage, three bedrooms, and 1½ baths for under $110,000.

Rockford has many good things going for it. Lowe's, the big home improvement company, decided to locate a new 1.4 million square foot regional distribution center there in 2006, and United Parcel Service (UPS) employs about 1,500 people at its 121,000 packages per hour sorting facility in Rockford. To round things out there are many service employers in the area: hospitals, the University of Illinois Medical School, shopping centers, and restaurants. They even have a UHL (United Hockey League) team, the Rockford *Ice Hogs*. About thirteen miles down the road in Belvidere, IL, Chrysler has a large manufacturing facility that employs about 2,700 workers.

Before I started doing my research I had never been to Rockford and I knew virtually nothing about it. I took a couple of weeks to research the greater Chicagoland area on the internet, which is how I found out about it. I took a drive up, liked what I saw, so I started looking at properties there. I looked at about fifteen properties over the course of three weekends and settled on an 1,850 square foot, 4-bedroom, 1¾ bath property that had been on the market for a total of 170 days.

It was originally listed for $117,900. The price was dropped to $114,900 and then to $109,900. When I came upon it, the price had just been dropped to $104,900. The property was actually worth about $108,000 - $110,000, but because it was initially priced incorrectly it had sat on the market so long that buyer's assumed there was something wrong with it and they stopped going to see it. Had they priced it at $109,900 to start with I suspect that they would have sold it in a few weeks.

As it was, I ended up writing an offer for $102,000 and I asked that the seller provide me with a thirteen month home warranty plan to cover all of the appliances and mechanicals, as well as a credit back at closing of $5,000 towards closing costs. Along with my offer I submitted a $3,000 earnest money check to show the seller that I was serious (In Rockford, 3% earnest money is the norm. In Chicago, 10% is the norm. You should submit whatever amount is appropriate for your particular market).

After some back and forth negotiating between the seller and I we ultimately agreed upon a price of $103,000 and I got the $5,000 credit and home warranty plan that I had asked for. That is a final net price of $98,000 ($103,000 – $5,000 = $98,000) which is about 10% below market value. Going into the negotiations I had set a net price of $100,000 as my absolute highest, so I came away $2,000 below what I would have been willing to pay. It was a successful negotiation.

Because I am a licensed agent, I got a commission of 3% on the sale, which was another $3,000 back to me. When all was said and done I bought a property worth about $108,000 for $95,000. The only difference between me and you is the fact that I am an agent and I got the extra commission. You would have got $5,000 back instead of $8,000 – still not bad at all.

Keep in mind that when I say that I "got back" $8,000, what I mean is that I got a credit towards the closing costs of $5,000 and a commission of $3,000. The total closing costs for this property were about $3,200 and the homeowner's insurance policy was about $900, so in the end I actually walked away from the closing table with my closing costs paid, a free thirteen month home warranty, my insurance paid, and a cash credit of about $900. When you figure in the seller credit for real estate taxes, I got a check at closing of about $3,500. Had you done this deal, you would have walked away with everything I did except the commission check.

**Return of Earnest Money at Closing**

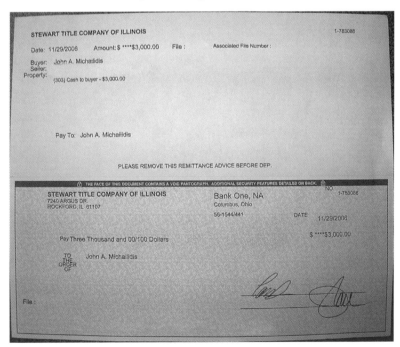

**Commission at Closing (Because I'm a Licensed Broker)**

**Credits (Cash Back) at Closing**

Just like magic, I own a house that I paid nothing for, and I got back checks totaling about $9,400 in the process! God bless America! I created a money machine! All that I needed to get the ball rolling was the $3,000 earnest money check, all of which was returned to me at closing, because I went with a 100% financing program.

By the way, I don't want you to think that the loan I got was some special program for sophisticated investors or people with stellar credit scores. Anyone with a credit score of 650 or higher could have qualified for this loan program. While a qualifying score of 650 is good, by no means is it considered "perfect credit."

✦ ✦ ✦

Interestingly enough, after my offer was accepted I found out about a drama that had been playing itself out behind the scenes during the negotiating process and of which I knew nothing about at the time. Remember what I told you about rehabbing properties and how difficult it can be? Well as it turns out, the property had been bought by a rehabber a few months before I got it. He put in all new carpeting. He refinished all of the wood flooring. He put in a new dishwasher, built-in microwave, refrigerator, stove, and kitchen cabinets. He updated the bathroom. He painted. There was a new hot-water heater and a new gas-forced-air heating unit. The inside of the place was like new!

But wait! The guy that I bought the house from was not the rehabber. I bought it from the guy that had lent the rehabber the money to buy the property. Because he had spent so much money on the rehab job, the original buyer was forced to price the property above market value if he hoped to make a profit. Unfortunately for him, 170 days later he found himself out of money and without a sale, so he was forced to give the deed to the property to the guy who had lent him the money, which is who I bought the house from.

I swear that I had no idea that any of this was going on when I made my offer, but I couldn't have asked for a better example of both the pitfalls and rewards that I have tried to teach you. By following the *WealthLoop* principles and looking at nice properties in nice neighborhoods that had been on the market for an above average length of time, I was able to find a motivated seller who was willing to give me a great deal. I told you that the *WealthLoop* principles work!

The first thing that I did after my offer was accepted was to hire a certified home inspector. Because I did not have any contacts in Rockford, I asked the listing agent for the property to provide me with a couple of recommendations. I made the calls and selected an inspector that I felt comfortable with.

Just the same, I had thoroughly looked the property over myself prior to making my offer and I already knew of two easily correctable issues that I wanted to address after the closing, which is why I requested a $5,000 credit from the seller when my closing costs were only about $3,200. I was looking for the inspector to point out any possible problems that I might have missed. The inspector and I spent about three hours going over every inch of the property with a fine-toothed comb and in the end there were no surprises and I was satisfied with its condition. The peace of mind that comes with a home inspection is well worth the $275 it cost me.

The next thing that I did was to order my sign and set up the following 24-hr recorded "800" number message:

*Hello and thank you for calling on this beautiful rent-to-own property located in a quiet, family neighborhood* *at 123 Green St. in Rockford. The two words that best describe this lovely home are SIZE and VALUE. At 1,850 square feet and having 4 bedrooms, 1¾ baths, living room, eat-in kitchen, family room with vaulted ceilings, a large finished basement, and attached garage, this house has all of the room you are likely to need and more. You get plenty of value because the house has been completely redone with fresh paint throughout, new carpeting, gleaming wood floors, new kitchen cabinets and appliances including a dishwasher and built-in microwave, and updated bathroom. You won't have to worry about maintenance problems because the appliances are new, as is the hot water heater and gas forced air heating unit. Did I mention that the house has central air conditioning? One look at this beautiful home and you'll want to move right in! We are having an open house on Saturday morning between 11:00 am and 11:45 am. Feel free to come on by, and if you like it be prepared to fill out an application. We are offering easy owner financing with rent-to-own terms, so don't be shy if your credit is less than perfect— it's okay. Just the same, we do require a complete credit and background check of all applicants, so please be prepared to submit a $35 money-order or cash application fee, or we won't be able to pay for the processing of your application. Thanks for calling and we look forward to financing you into this fabulous family home!*

I got permission from the seller to put my sign in the window before we closed on the property, so two weeks after my offer was accepted and two weeks before the scheduled closing I drove up to Rockford and put up the sign. I was encouraged when the first sign call came in that same day. I also ordered a classified ad to be placed in the *Homes For Rent* section of the newspaper that following week. The paper's mandatory formatting guidelines kept me from setting the ad up exactly as I would have liked to, but it came out okay just the same:

Three days after the sign went up, the classified ad hit the paper, and by the day of the open house I had received 58 calls. By using the phone script to explain to callers that a complete background and credit check would be performed, and that they would need to submit a $35 application fee if they were interested in the property, I purposely attempted to *weed out* the most undesirable prospective tenants ahead of time. I only wanted to spend my time with the best prospective candidates, so I let the technology do the pre-screening for me.

Since the whole point of having an "800" number is to direct pre-screened candidates to the property without having to explain everything to them prior to their visit, I drove up to the open house on Saturday morning not knowing exactly how many people would show up. In preparation for the open-house I had gotten a card-table and a couple of folding chairs ready, my portable radio, as well as a supply of sign-in sheets, rent-to-own worksheets, tenant evaluation questionnaires, and application forms. I had practiced my *presentation* in the mirror several times, so that I felt confident that I wouldn't mess it up when I finally got in front of a real prospective tenant/buyer, and I practiced filling out the forms ahead of time.

To make a long story short, I had nine people come by and five of the nine were clearly interested. In talking to them I quickly realized that two of the five could not afford to purchase the property, and another two of the five had proved themselves to be unworthy of further discussion, because they had failed to follow the instructions to be prepared to submit an application fee. The fifth party had followed instructions and handed me $35 cash.

I went over the rent-to-own program with them and I explained that I only wanted serious people who were committed to purchase the property. I explained to them that I would be taking a risk if I agreed to work with them, and I let them know that they should seriously consider their motivation, because if they signed up for the program and failed to follow through they would be loosing all of their up-front money and all of their rent credits. I made them tell me all of the reasons why they wanted the property and why I should take a chance on them.

I let them know that in order for them to qualify for the property they would need to put up a minimum of $5,000 up-front plus the first month's rent, but that they might need to put up even more depending on the outcome of their credit report and background checks. They told me that they understood and that they would be able to come up with as much as $15,000 if need be.

I explained to them that I estimated the current value of the property to be $108,000. I explained to them that the option price that they would be paying for the house in three years was the current valuation of $108,000 plus an assumed annual appreciation of 4% per year. They agreed with those terms, so I proceeded to go over three different rental payment options for them to consider. By noon they had completed the application and I was on my way.

Up to that point I felt good about them as prospective tenant/buyers. They were a middle aged couple and their elderly mother was living with them. They had started business three months prior, which meant that they could not show the steady, long-term income that a bank would require for a mortgage. They were honest with me and told me that due to some prior irresponsibility their credit was not the greatest.

In their favor was the fact that their particular type of business required them to have undergone a rigorous background screening in order to receive a state license – the fact that they did get the state license was a plus as far as I was concerned. They also told me that their business was doing well and that they had secured several long-term contracts. Finally, they told me that they were very serious about wanting the property and that they would be willing to make up to a $15,000 up-front option payment on the property.

I ran both of their credit and background reports and their credit reports were as expected. More important to me however was the fact that their criminal background checks came back clear. I called them back and told them that given the circumstances I would not need their full $15,000 up front, but that I would need $7,500 plus the first month's rent. They were happy to get the good news and they told me that they had decided to take the $1,500 per month rental option, so that they could maximize their credits. We met later in the week and they gave me a $2,500 deposit to hold the property.

**Tenant/Buyer's Initial Deposit**

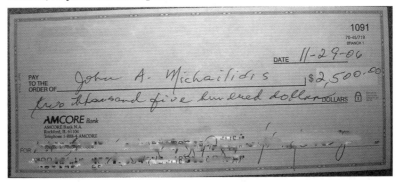

This is what the deal looks like on paper from the tenant/buyer's perspective. They decided to go with option #3.

## Tenant/Buyer Rental Options

|  | Option 1 | Option 2 | Option3 |
|---|---|---|---|
| Monthly Rent: | $ 1,200 | $ 1,350 | $ 1,500 |
| Monthly Rent Credit: | $ 100 | $ 300 | $ 500 |
| 36-month Rent Credit: | $ 3,600 | $ 10,800 | $ 18,000 |
| Purchase Price: | $121,500 | $ 121,500 | $121,500 |
| Rent Credit: | <$3,600> | <$10,800> | <$18,000> |
| Up-front Payment: | <$7,500> | <$ 7,500> | <$ 7,500> |
| Final Tenant Price: | $110,400 | $ 103,200 | $ 96,000 |
| Accrued Tenant Equity $: | $ 11,100 | $ 18,300 | $ 25,500 |
| Accrued Tenant Equity %: | 9% | 15% | 21% |

This is a perfect example of the kind of win-win transactions that you can hope to engage in using the *WealthLoop* principles for personal wealth creation through residential real estate investing. The buyer wins in a big way, because they get the opportunity to build a large equity stake in a very nice house that, due to their poor credit history, they would have no way of purchasing conventionally. So long as they keep up the payments and don't get themselves in any more financial trouble, in a mere 36 months they will be the proud owners of a very nice home.

The seller wins in a big way, because he gets almost ten months worth of mortgage payments up front, plus a positive monthly cash-flow of about $420 dollars a month! Also, because I set up the rental agreement according to the principles taught in the *WealthLoop* system, the tenant is responsible for the first $250 per month of any repairs that might be necessary. In the end, I created a $30,000 return over 36-months out of thin air!

**Tenant/Buyer's Final Option Money Deposit**

Take a look at what this deal looks like on paper from the seller's perspective:

## Cash-Flow Worksheet:

Property Value: $108,000

Purchase Price: $ 98,000 (after credits)

Loan Amount: <$103,000>

Credits
& Commission: $ 8,000

Closing Costs
& Insurance: <$ 4,100>

Improvements
After Closing: <$ 3,000>

Initial Closing
Cash Received: $ 900 (a)

Monthly
Loan Payment: $ 775

Monthly Property
Tax Payment: $ 230

Monthly PMI: $ 0

Monthly Property
Insurance: $ 75

Total Monthly
Payment: $ 1,080

Monthly Rental
Income: $ 1,500

Monthly Positive
Cash Flow: $ 420 (b)

Up-Front
Payment From
Tenant/Buyer: $ 7,500 (c)

### Tax Benefit Calculation:

| | |
|---|---|
| Annual Insurance x 3yrs | $ 2,700 |
| Property Tax x 3yrs | $ 8,280 |
| Mortgage Interest x 3yrs | $ 27,900 |
| Total Expense Deduction | $ 38,880 |
| Assumed Tax Rate | 30% |
| Tax Benefit | $ 11,664 |

## 36-Month Sale Worksheet:

Sale Price: $121,500

– Up-front
Payment
Credit <$ 7,500>

– Total Monthly
Rent Credits: <$ 18,000>

– Loan Payoff: <$100,300>

– Closing Costs <$ 1,000>

Net From Sale: <$ 5,300>

+ Initial Closing
Cash to Seller: $ 900 (a)

+ Cash Flow: $ 15,120 (b)

+ Up-Front
Payment: $ 7,500 (c)

+ Tax Benefit: $ 11,664

Total Return
Before Taxes: $ 29,884

NOTE: Because I did not put any money down on this property it is impossible to calculate a percentage rate of return—the rate of return is infinite! In effect, I created $30,000 out of thin air! Also, to keep things simple for you I didn't even figure the depreciation expense deduction into the tax benefit, which boosts the return even further.

\* The above is for illustrative purposes only. Always check with a tax professional regarding your own tax situation.

So, there you have it. This is not rocket science. YOU can do this if you want to. The question is, "Do you really want to?" The choice is yours and yours alone—I cannot make it for you. You hold in your hands the golden keys to personal wealth creation, but you must TAKE ACTION NOW! Welcome to the *WealthLoop . . .*

**Tenant/Buyer's 1st Month Rent**

# Chapter 20

## Forms, Checklists and Resources

---

**DISCLAIMER**

Every state, and many municipalities, have their own requirements with respect to leases and other real estate agreements.

The agreements shown herein are for
**EXAMPLE PURPOSES ONLY**
and should NOT be used without first consulting with a qualified legal professional to determine their applicability to your situation. Neither the author, nor publisher assumes any liability with respect to the use of these forms or agreements.

---

Here you will find forms and checklists for each phase of the *WealthLoop* system—locating properties, negotiating offers and purchasing properties, and finding and signing up tenant/buyers. Every time you work through a rent-to-own-deal you should have the checklists in front of you so that you do not miss any crucial details. Also, I hope that you will treat these forms and checklists as an integral part of the book by reading through them now and becoming intimately familiar with their content.

Included is an "Option To Purchase" agreement, which is the type of form that you will be using, in conjunction with a standard lease agreement, to set up your rent-to-own deals with tenant/buyers. Read through it several times so that you completely understand its provisions. It is the key to putting together rent-to-own deals.

An option agreement is ALWAYS used in conjunction with a lease agreement—never alone! The lease sets out the agreement with respect to the rental aspects of the deal and the option agreement sets out the purchase aspects of the deal. Unless you use both types of agreements together you will not have put together a valid rent-to-own transaction.

Leases tend to be fairly straightforward documents that many people are familiar with, if for no other reason than they themselves have rented in the past. Nevertheless, so that you can familiarize yourself with many of the issues typically addressed in such an agreement, I have included a sample lease for you to read. The example lease included here is what I would call a "long form" version, which means that it includes many clauses that might not be absolutely necessary. Many investors get by with a much shorter lease form, but I wanted to give you some good reading.

Understand that I do not expect you to use the lease example provided without first checking with a competent real estate advisor to determine its legality and applicability for your area. Check around (ask your real estate agent) to find a lease agreement that is typical of those used in your area and familiarize yourself with its provisions.

Here is what you will find in this section:

1. Property Evaluation Checklist
2. Financial Evaluation Worksheet
3. Post-Offer Checklist
4. Open House Sign-In Sheet
5. Prospective Tenant Rent-to-Own Worksheet
6. Tenant Evaluation Questionnaire
7. Rental Application Form
8. Deposit to Hold Property Form
9. Sample Residential Lease Agreement
10. Sample Option To Purchase Agreement

A companion CD is available for purchase that contains all of the above checklists and forms as both Microsoft Word and PDF files. Having the forms and checklists on CD will allow you to modify them to suit your specific needs and to save and print them as needed.

There are also several things on the CD that I was just not able to get into the book. There is a Microsoft Excel spreadsheet that has been set up to help you analyze the numbers for the rent-to-own deals you are putting together. There are also several sample ads that have proven to be successful, and there is a script that you can use for your 800 number recorded message. Finally, the CD contains sample dialogue that you can use when negotiating with both sellers and prospective tenant/buyers.

All in all, the companion CD is full of valuable information that will make your investing life easier. While not absolutely necessary for you to get started, the companion CD will make it easier for you to organize and keep track of your investing progress and the additional information and scripts will save you a lot of trial and error. To make it worth your while, and to express my gratitude to you for having purchased the book, the companion CD also includes two FREE bonuses for readers of the book.

The first FREE bonus for book readers who order the CD is a thirty-minute audio interview in which I explain my investing philosophy and the *WealthLoop* system's finer points. Sometimes information just sticks better if you hear it rather than reading it. I have received enthusiastic comments from listeners who found the audio interview to be most helpful with respect to clarifying certain points of the *WealthLoop* system and many have found it to be the motivating push they needed to hear in order to get started. It makes for great listening material in your car while riding through neighborhoods checking out properties.

The second FREE bonus for book readers who order the companion Forms CD is a complimentary copy of my context rich quarterly *WealthLoop Financial Freedom Newsletter.* The newsletter typically features explanations of advanced investing techniques, investing tips and advice, a question/answer section, interesting quotes and interviews, as well as a section on real world investing stories from the trenches.

You can find order forms for both the companion Forms CD and the newsletter subscription at the back of the book, or you can order either or both directly from the website at www.WealthLoop.com.

# Property Evaluation Checklist

(Rate each category from 1–4, with 1 being excellent and 4 being poor)

| Property Evaluation Checklist | Property #1 | Property #2 | Property #3 |
|---|---|---|---|
| Address | | | |
| Asking Price | $ | $ | $ |
| Monthly Rent Comparables  (3) | $    /    / | $    /    / | $    /    / |
| **Neighborhood Ranking** | | | |
| Proximity to Schools | 1  2  3  4 | 1  2  3  4 | 1  2  3  4 |
| Proximity to Shopping | 1  2  3  4 | 1  2  3  4 | 1  2  3  4 |
| Proximity to Expressways | 1  2  3  4 | 1  2  3  4 | 1  2  3  4 |
| Proximity to Public Transportation | 1  2  3  4 | 1  2  3  4 | 1  2  3  4 |
| Condition of Streets/Sidewalks | 1  2  3  4 | 1  2  3  4 | 1  2  3  4 |
| Traffic Volume | 1  2  3  4 | 1  2  3  4 | 1  2  3  4 |
| Proximity to Parks/Recreation | 1  2  3  4 | 1  2  3  4 | 1  2  3  4 |
| Condition of Adjacent Properties | 1  2  3  4 | 1  2  3  4 | 1  2  3  4 |
| Environmental Concerns/Influences | 1  2  3  4 | 1  2  3  4 | 1  2  3  4 |
| **Exterior** | | | |
| Approximate Age | 1  2  3  4 | 1  2  3  4 | 1  2  3  4 |
| Roof Condition | 1  2  3  4 | 1  2  3  4 | 1  2  3  4 |
| Foundation Condition | 1  2  3  4 | 1  2  3  4 | 1  2  3  4 |
| Condition of Fences | 1  2  3  4 | 1  2  3  4 | 1  2  3  4 |
| Condition of Landscaping | 1  2  3  4 | 1  2  3  4 | 1  2  3  4 |
| Garage Condition | 1  2  3  4 | 1  2  3  4 | 1  2  3  4 |
| Condition of Windows/Frames | 1  2  3  4 | 1  2  3  4 | 1  2  3  4 |
| Storm Windows/Screens | 1  2  3  4 | 1  2  3  4 | 1  2  3  4 |
| Garage Size (# Cars) | 1  2  3  4 | 1  2  3  4 | 1  2  3  4 |
| **Interior** | | | |
| # Bathrooms | | | |
| Condition of Bathrooms | 1  2  3  4 | 1  2  3  4 | 1  2  3  4 |
| # Bedrooms | | | |
| Condition of Bedrooms | 1  2  3  4 | 1  2  3  4 | 1  2  3  4 |
| Condition of Living Room | 1  2  3  4 | 1  2  3  4 | 1  2  3  4 |
| Fireplace | Y  N | Y  N | Y  N |
| Separate Dining Room | Y  N | Y  N | Y  N |
| Condition of Flooring | 1  2  3  4 | 1  2  3  4 | 1  2  3  4 |
| Condition of Kitchen | 1  2  3  4 | 1  2  3  4 | 1  2  3  4 |
| Laundry Space | Y  N | Y  N | Y  N |
| Finished Basement | Y  N | Y  N | Y  N |
| Condition of Basement | 1  2  3  4 | 1  2  3  4 | 1  2  3  4 |
| **Appliances/Mechanicals** | | | |
| Condition of Refrigerator | 1  2  3  4 | 1  2  3  4 | 1  2  3  4 |
| Condition of Stove/Oven (Gas/Electric) | 1  2  3  4 | 1  2  3  4 | 1  2  3  4 |
| Garbage Disposal | Y  N | Y  N | Y  N |
| Condition of Dishwasher | 1  2  3  4 | 1  2  3  4 | 1  2  3  4 |
| Type of  Heat | | | |
| Condition of Heating Unit | 1  2  3  4 | 1  2  3  4 | 1  2  3  4 |
| Condition of Hot Water Heater | 1  2  3  4 | 1  2  3  4 | 1  2  3  4 |
| Central Air Conditioning | Y  N | Y  N | Y  N |
| Condition of Air Conditioning | 1  2  3  4 | 1  2  3  4 | 1  2  3  4 |
| **Overall Rating** | | | |
| Exterior Structure | 1  2  3  4 | 1  2  3  4 | 1  2  3  4 |
| Exterior Grounds | 1  2  3  4 | 1  2  3  4 | 1  2  3  4 |
| Interior Layout | 1  2  3  4 | 1  2  3  4 | 1  2  3  4 |
| Interior Condition | 1  2  3  4 | 1  2  3  4 | 1  2  3  4 |
| Appliances/Mechanicals | 1  2  3  4 | 1  2  3  4 | 1  2  3  4 |

## Financial Evaluation Worksheet

### I. Rent Comparables Worksheet:

|  | Comp 1 | Comp 2 | Comp 3 |
|---|---|---|---|
| Address: | | | |
| $ Rent/m: | | | |
| #Bed: | | | |
| #Bath: | | | |
| Finished Bsmt? | | | |
| #Car Garage: | | | |

### II. Cash-Flow Worksheet:

Property Value:       $
Purchase Price:       $
Loan Amount:       $
Down Payment:       $
Closing Costs:       $

**Out Of Pocket
Amount:       $**

Monthly
Loan Payment:       $

Monthly Property
Tax Payment:       $

Monthly PMI:       $

Monthly Property
Insurance:       $

Miscellaneous:       $

Total Monthly
Payment:       $

Monthly Rental
Income:       $

**Monthly Positive
Cash Flow:       $**

**Up-Front
Payment From
Tenant/Buyer:       $**

### III. After Sale Worksheet:

Sale Price:       $

– Up-front
   Payment       $

– Total
   Rent Credits:       $

– Loan Payoff:       $

– Closing Costs       $

Net From Sale:       $

+ Cash Flow:       $

+ Up-Front
   Payment:       $

+ Tax Benefit:       $

Total Return:       $

## Post-Offer Checklist

### After Acceptance/Prior to Closing

❏ Acceptable inspection results? Possibly ask for a credit to fix previously unknown defects.

❏ If you have a tenant/buyer waiting list, notify list that you will be accepting applications for a new rent-to-own property coming available.

❏ Designate and record a mailbox number (ID#) on your 800-hotline system for this property.

❏ Order a sign with the 800 number and ID# for this property.

### After Closing

❏ Place sign in yard.

❏ Thoroughly clean property, paint if needed, minor repairs if needed, manicure yard.

❏ Schedule open houses.

❏ Place classified ad in local newspaper.

❏ Print supply of applications/forms as needed.

❏ Check your attitude for signs of weakness. Control the renting process and do not let the tenant/buyer(s) control you. Never accept an application without a $35 fee. Only accept cash, certified funds, or money orders. Always check employment, landlord, credit references, and criminal background.

## Open House Sign-In Sheet

| | Name | Phone# | E-mail | Max. Up-front Pmt. $ Available | How did you hear about us? |
|---|---|---|---|---|---|
| 1. | | | | | |
| 2. | | | | | |
| 3. | | | | | |
| 4. | | | | | |
| 5. | | | | | |
| 6. | | | | | |
| 7. | | | | | |
| 8. | | | | | |
| 9. | | | | | |
| 10. | | | | | |
| 11. | | | | | |
| 12. | | | | | |
| 13. | | | | | |
| 14. | | | | | |
| 15. | | | | | |
| 16. | | | | | |
| 17. | | | | | |

## Prospective Tenant Rent-To-Own Worksheet

|  | Option 1 | | Option 2 | | Option3 | |
|---|---|---|---|---|---|---|
| Monthly Rent: | $ | | $ | | $ | |
| Monthly Rent Credit: | $ | | $ | | $ | |
| Annual Rent Credit: | $ | | $ | | $ | |
| __ Month Purchase Price: | $ | | $ | | $ | |
| __ Month Rent Credit: | <$ | > | <$ | > | <$ | > |
| Up-front Payment: | <$ | > | <$ | > | <$ | > |
| Final Tenant Price: | $ | | $ | | $ | |

**Here's Why Renting-to-Own Makes Sense:**

1. **Build Equity Fast:** With a conventional mortgage only a few dollars a month goes towards equity – most of your payments go towards interest. Renting-to-own builds equity faster!

2. **Avoid Bank Hassles:** Unless you have good credit to start with, renting-to-own may be your only realistic opportunity to own your own home in the near future.

3. **Build Credit:** By living up to your agreement and paying your rent on time you build a strong, positive credit history that can benefit you into the future.

4. **Flexible Options:** Unlike bank financing, renting-to-own gives you the option of purchasing the property—without the obligation!

## Tenant Evaluation Questionnaire

It is extremely important that you ask the prospective tenant/buyer each and every question point-blank. Once you ask the question, you MUST KEEP YOUR MOUTH SHUT and listen to the answer. (Very important: even if there is dead silence, say nothing until they have answered.)

It is also extremely important that you call ALL present and former employers and landlords and ask them point-blank if they think the prospective tenant/buyer(s) is a responsible person who is worthy of the opportunity you are giving them.

1. What do you love about the property and why do you want to own it?

2. What is the absolute most money that you can invest up-front to purchase the property?

3. How do you intend to come up with that money?
   (It's in the bank/Borrow it/Next paycheck/etc.)

4. When I call your previous landlords, what will they tell me about their experience with you?

5. When I look at your credit report, what will I find?
   Do you know your credit score?

6. When I do a criminal background check, what will I find?

7. When I speak with your previous employers, what will they have to say about you?

8. Why are you unable to get a bank loan to buy the property outright?

9. Why do you want to own your own home?

10. Do you completely and fully understand that I only want to work with people who are 100% committed to purchasing this home from me, and that there will be absolutely no refund whatsoever, no matter what, if you decide not to go through with the deal?

# Rental Application

Equal Housing Opportunity

The undersigned hereby makes an application to rent the property located at: _____
_____

**To guarantee compliance with the Federal Fair Housing Acts, a separate application and a nonrefundable $35.00 processing fee is required.**

Current monthly rent payment $_____ Date you would like to move _____
Applicant #1: monthly income $_____ Applicant #2: monthly income $_____

## PLEASE TELL US ABOUT YOURSELF

Full Name _____ Home Phone (     ) _____
Date of Birth _____ Social Security # _____
Drivers License State _____ Drivers License # _____
Email Address: _____(optional) Other Phone (     ) _____

Full Name _____ Home Phone (     ) _____
Date of Birth _____ Social Security # _____
Drivers License State _____ Drivers License # _____
Email Address: _____(optional) Other Phone (     ) _____

Names of Dependents                                    Date of Birth
_____
_____
_____

List All Pets _____

## PLEASE GIVE RESIDENTIAL HISTORY (LAST 3 YEARS)

**Current Address** _____ Apt# _____
City _____ State _____ Zip _____
Month/Year Moved In _____Month/Year Moved Out _____
Reasons for Leaving _____ Rent $ _____
Owner/Agent Name _____Phone (     ) _____

**Previous Address** _____ Apt# _____
City _____ State _____ Zip _____
Month/Year Moved In _____Month/Year Moved Out _____
Reasons for Leaving _____ Rent $ _____
Owner/Agent Name _____Phone (     ) _____

**Previous Address** _____ Apt# _____
City _____ State _____ Zip _____
Month/Year Moved In _____Month/Year Moved Out _____
Reasons for Leaving _____ Rent $ _____
Owner/Agent Name _____Phone (     ) _____

**Previous Address** _____ Apt# _____
City _____ State _____ Zip _____
Month/Year Moved In _____Month/Year Moved Out _____
Reasons for Leaving _____ Rent $ _____
Owner/Agent Name _____Phone (     ) _____

## PLEASE DESCRIBE YOUR CREDIT HISTORY

Have you declared bankruptcy in the past seven (7) years?          Yes _____ No _____
Have you ever been evicted from a rental residence?               Yes _____ No _____
Have you had two or more late rental payments in the past year? (Credit is checked.
Perfect credit not expected, but perfect honesty ALWAYS is.)     Yes _____ No _____
Have you ever willfully or intentionally refused to pay rent when due?   Yes _____ No _____

## PLEASE PROVIDE YOUR EMPLOYMENT INFORMATION

**Applicant Status:** _____ Full Time _____ Part Time _____ Student _____Unemployed
**Primary Applicant's Employer Name** _____
Address _____
Month/Year Hired _____ Month/Year Left _____
Your Job Title/Description _____
Supervisor's Name/Title _____ Phone ( ) _____
Monthly Take-Home Pay $ _____ (If employed by above less than 12 months, give
name & phone of previous employer or schools below).

**Primary Applicant's Prior Employer Name** _____
Address _____
Month/Year Hired _____ Month/Year Left _____
Your Job Title/Description _____
Supervisor's Name/Title _____ Phone ( ) _____
Monthly Take-Home Pay $ _____ (If employed by above less than 12 months, give
name & phone of previous employer or schools below).

**Co-Applicant Status:** _____ Full Time _____ Part Time _____ Student _____Unemployed
**Co-Applicant's Employer Name** _____
Address _____
Month/Year Hired _____ Month/Year Left _____
Your Job Title/Description _____
Supervisor's Name/Title _____ Phone ( ) _____
Monthly Take-Home Pay $ _____ (If employed by above less than 12 months, give
name & phone of previous employer or schools below).

**Co-Applicant's Prior Employer Name** _____
Address _____
Month/Year Hired _____ Month/Year Left _____
Your Job Title/Description _____
Supervisor's Name/Title _____ Phone ( ) _____
Monthly Take-Home Pay $ _____ (If employed by above less than 12 months, give
name & phone of previous employer or schools below).

If you have other sources of income that you would like us to consider, please list income, source, and person (banker, employer, etc.) whom we may contact for confirmation. You do not have to reveal alimony, child support, or spouse's annual income unless you want us to consider it in this application.

Amount $ _____ Source/Contact Name _____
Phone ( ) _____

Amount $ _____ Source/Contact Name _____
Phone ( ) _____

164

## PLEASE LIST YOUR REFERENCES

### Bank Accounts
Name _____ Type of Account _____ Account Number _____
Name _____ Type of Account _____ Account Number _____

### Personal Reference or Emergency Contact
Name _____ Address _____
Phone _____ Relationship _____

**Vehicle Information:** Make/Model _____ Year _____ License _____ State _____

## ADDITIONAL INFORMATION:
Please give any additional information that might help owner/management evaluate this application?

_____
_____
_____
_____
_____
_____

Where may we reach you to discuss this application?

Day Phone # (     ) _____Night Phone # (     ) _____

The above information, to the best of my knowledge, is true and correct.

Please Print Name _____
Please sign  X _____
　　　　　　　　Primary Applicant　　　　　　　　　　　　Date

Please Print Name _____
Please sign  X _____
　　　　　　　　Co-Applicant　　　　　　　　　　　　　Date

## AUTHORIZATION
### Release of Information

I authorize an investigation of my police record, credit, tenant history, banking and employment for the purposes of renting a house, apartment, or condo from this owner/manager.

Applicant Name (please print) _____

X _____
　　　　　　　Signature　　　　　　　　　　　　　　　Date

Co-Applicant Name (please print) _____

X _____
　　　　　　　Signature　　　　　　　　　　　　　　　Date

### APPLICANT:  PLEASE DO NOT WRITE BELOW  (FOR OFFICE USE ONLY)

Deposit of $ _____ Received by _____ Date _____

OFFICE NOTES:

## Deposit to Hold Property

Prospective Tenant _____

is/are depositing $ _____ to hold position in order to rent-to-own the
property located at: _____

The deposit will be paid as follows: _____

All prospective Tenant(s) deposits are "option consideration" and will be applied towards the purchase of the above named property, provided that prospective Tenant(s) complies with all terms and conditions of the RESIDENTIAL LEASE AGREEMENT and OPTION TO PURCHASE AGREEMENT that may be entered into.

This deposit, and any future deposits, are NON-REFUNDABLE, with prospective Tenant(s) being responsible for paying an additional deposit (option consideration) of $ _____ on or before _____. Before moving into the property on _____ _____, and in addition to the above named deposit(s), Tenant(s) must pay Landlord the first month's rent of $_____. If either of these payments are not received by Landlord on the dates specified herein, the Landlord may, at the Landlord's sole discretion, cancel the agreement with prospective Tenant(s) and all monies paid to Landlord by said Tenant(s) will be kept as liquidated damages to cover application review, marketing costs to fill the property, and lost opportunities to enter into an agreement with another prospective Tenant(s).

This agreement is subject to the Landlord's final approval of the prospective Tenant(s) application. In the event that the Landlord does not approve the Tenant(s) application, and at the Landlord's sole discretion, Landlord may refund all of the deposit (less a $250 handling fee) and cancel any agreements that may have been entered into.

Prospective Tenant(s) understands that NO VALID LEASE OR OPTION EXISTS until all payments described herein have been paid to and accepted by Landlord, and the RESIDENTIAL LEASE AGREEMENT and OPTION TO PURCHASE AGREEMENT have been completed and signed by the parties.

To be accepted, all payments must be in the form of either certified funds or money order, and in no case will Tenant/Buyer(s) be permitted to enter/occupy the premises before the specified occupancy date, and until all funds have been received, cleared the bank, and been deposited into Landlord's account.

LANDLORD

Sign: _____ Print: _____ Date: _____

TENANT(S)

Sign: _____ Print: _____ Date: _____

Sign: _____ Print: _____ Date: _____

# Residential Lease Agreement

THIS LEASE AGREEMENT (hereinafter referred to as the "Agreement") made and entered into this _____ day of _____ , 20 _____, by and between _____ (hereinafter referred to as "Landlord") and _____ (hereinafter referred to as "Tenant").

WHEREAS, Landlord is the fee owner of certain real property having a street address of

_____

(hereinafter referred to as the "Premises").

WHEREAS, Landlord desires to lease the Premises to Tenant upon the terms and conditions as contained herein;

WHEREAS, Tenant desires to lease the Premises from Landlord on the terms and conditions as contained herein;

NOW, THEREFORE, for and in consideration of the covenants and obligations contained herein and other good and valuable consideration, the receipt and sufficiency of which is hereby acknowledged, the parties hereto hereby agree as follows:

1. **TERM.** Landlord leases to Tenant and Tenant leases from Landlord the above described Premises together with any and all appurtenances thereto, for a term of _____ [specify number of months or years], such term beginning on _____, and ending at 12 o'clock midnight on _____.

2. **RENT.** The rent for the term hereof is the monthly sum of _____ DOLLARS ($_____) payable on the _____day of each month of the term, first and last installments to be paid upon the due execution of this Agreement, the second installment to be paid on _____. All such payments shall be made to Landlord at Landlord's address as set forth in the preamble to this Agreement on or before the due date and without demand.

3. **SECURITY DEPOSIT.** Upon the due execution of this Agreement, Tenant shall deposit with Landlord the sum of _____ DOLLARS ($_____) receipt of which is hereby acknowledged by Landlord, as security for any damage caused to the Premises during the term hereof.

4. **USE OF PREMISES.** The Premises shall be used and occupied by Tenant and Tenant's immediate family, consisting of _____ _____ _____, exclusively, as a private single-family dwelling, and no part of the Premises shall be used at any time during the term of this Agreement by Tenant for the purpose of carrying on any business, profession, or trade of any kind, or for any purpose other than as a private single-family dwelling. Tenant shall not allow any other person, other than Tenant's immediate family or transient relatives and friends who are guests of Tenant, to use or occupy the Premises without first obtaining Landlord's written consent to such use. Tenant shall comply with any and all laws, ordinances, rules and orders of any and all governmental or quasi-governmental authorities affecting the cleanliness, use, occupancy and preservation of the Premises.

5. **CONDITION OF PREMISES.** Tenant stipulates, represents and warrants that Tenant has examined the Premises and that they are at the time of this Lease in good order, repair, and in a safe, clean and tenantable condition.

6. **ASSIGNMENT AND SUB-LETTING.** Tenant shall not assign this Agreement, or sub-let or grant any license to use the Premises or any part thereof without the prior written consent of Landlord. A consent by Landlord to one such assignment, sub-letting or license shall not be deemed to be a consent to any subsequent assignment, sub-letting or license. An assignment, sub-letting or license without the prior written consent of Landlord or an assignment or sub-letting by operation of law shall be absolutely null and void and shall, at Landlord's option, terminate this Agreement.

7. **ALTERATIONS AND IMPROVEMENTS.** Tenant shall make no alterations to the buildings or improvements on the Premises or construct any building or make any other improvements on the Premises without the prior written consent of Landlord. Any and all alterations, changes, and/or improvements built, constructed or placed on the Premises by Tenant shall, unless otherwise provided by written agreement between Landlord and Tenant, be and become the property of Landlord and remain on the Premises at the expiration or earlier termination of this Agreement.

8. **NON-DELIVERY OF POSSESSION.** In the event Landlord cannot deliver possession of the Premises to Tenant upon the commencement of the Lease term, through no fault of Landlord or its agents, then Landlord or its agents shall have no liability, but the rental herein provided shall abate until possession is given. Landlord or its agents shall have thirty (30) days in which to give possession, and if possession is tendered within such time, Tenant agrees to accept the demised Premises and pay the rental herein provided from that date. In the event possession cannot be delivered within such time, through no fault of Landlord or its agents, then this Agreement and all rights hereunder shall terminate.

9. **HAZARDOUS MATERIALS.** Tenant shall not keep on the Premises any item of a dangerous, flammable or explosive character that might unreasonably increase the danger of fire or explosion on the Premises or that might be considered hazardous or extra hazardous by any responsible insurance company.

10. **UTILITIES.** Tenant shall be responsible for arranging for and paying for all utility services required on the Premises, including, but not limited to water and sewer, natural gas, electricity, telephone, and trash removal.

11. **MAINTENANCE AND REPAIR; RULES.** Tenant will, at its sole expense, keep and maintain the Premises and appurtenances in good and sanitary condition and repair during the term of this Agreement and any renewal thereof. Without limiting the generality of the foregoing, Tenant shall:

    (a)    Not obstruct the driveways, sidewalks, courts, entryways, stairs and/or halls, which shall be used for the purposes of ingress and egress only;

    (b)    Keep all windows, glass, window coverings, doors, locks and hardware in good, clean order and repair;

    (c)    Not obstruct or cover the windows or doors;

(d)    Not leave windows or doors in an open position during any inclement weather;

(e)    Not hang any laundry, clothing, sheets, etc. from any window, rail, porch or balcony nor air or dry any of same within any yard area or space;

(f)    Not cause or permit any locks or hooks to be placed upon any door or window without the prior written consent of Landlord;

(g)    Keep all air conditioning filters clean and free from dirt;

(h)    Keep all lavatories, sinks, toilets, and all other water and plumbing apparatus in good order and repair and shall use same only for the purposes for which they were constructed. Tenant shall not allow any sweepings, rubbish, sand, rags, ashes or other substances to be thrown or deposited therein. Any damage to any such apparatus and the cost of clearing stopped plumbing resulting from misuse shall be borne by Tenant;

(i)    And Tenant's family and guests shall at all times maintain order in the Premises and at all places on the Premises, and shall not make or permit any loud or improper noises, or otherwise disturb other residents, or neighbors;

(j)    Keep all radios, television sets, stereos, phonographs, etc., turned down to a level of sound that does not annoy or interfere with other residents, or neighbors;

(k)    Deposit all trash, garbage, rubbish or refuse in the locations provided therefore and will not allow any trash, garbage, rubbish or refuse to be deposited or permitted to stand on the exterior of any building or within the common elements;

(l)    Abide by and be bound by any and all rules and regulations affecting the Premises or the common area appurtenant thereto which may be adopted or promulgated by the Condominium or Homeowners' Association having control over them.

12.    **DAMAGE TO PREMISES.**  In the event the Premises are destroyed or rendered wholly uninhabitable by fire, storm, earthquake, or other casualty not caused by the negligence of Tenant, this Agreement shall terminate from such time except for the purpose of enforcing rights that may have then accrued hereunder. The rental provided for herein shall then be accounted for by and between Landlord and Tenant up to the time of such injury or destruction of the Premises, Tenant paying rentals up to such date and Landlord refunding rentals collected beyond such date. Should a portion of the Premises thereby be rendered uninhabitable, the Landlord shall have the option of either repairing such injured or damaged portion or terminating this Lease. In the event that Landlord exercises its right to repair such uninhabitable portion, the rental shall abate in the proportion that the injured parts bear to the whole Premises, and such part so injured shall be restored by Landlord as speedily as practicable, after which the full rent shall recommence and the Agreement continue according to its terms.

13.    **INSPECTION OF PREMISES.**  Landlord and Landlord's agents shall have the right at all reasonable times during the term of this Agreement and any renewal thereof to enter the Premises for the purpose of inspecting the Premises and all buildings and improvements thereon. And for the purposes of making any repairs, additions, or altera-

tions, as may be deemed appropriate by Landlord for the preservation of the Premises or the building. Landlord and its agents shall further have the right to exhibit the Premises and to display the usual "for sale", "for rent" or "vacancy" signs on the Premises at any time within forty-five (45) days before the expiration of this Lease. The right of entry shall likewise exist for the purpose of removing placards, signs, fixtures, alterations or additions that do not conform to this Agreement or to any restrictions, rules or regulations affecting the Premises.

14. **SUBORDINATION OF LEASE.** This Agreement and Tenant's interest hereunder are and shall be subordinate, junior and inferior to any and all mortgages, liens or encumbrances now or hereafter placed on the Premises by Landlord, all advances made under any such mortgages, liens or encumbrances (including, but not limited to, future advances), the interest payable on such mortgages, liens or encumbrances and any and all renewals, extensions or modifications of such mortgages, liens or encumbrances.

15. **TENANT'S HOLD OVER.** If Tenant remains in possession of the Premises with the consent of Landlord after the natural expiration of this Agreement, a new tenancy from month-to-month shall be created between Landlord and Tenant which shall be subject to all of the terms and conditions hereof except that rent shall then be due and owing at _____ DOLLARS ($ _____) per month and except that such tenancy shall be terminable upon fifteen (15) days written notice served by either party.

16. **SURRENDER OF PREMISES.** Upon the expiration of the term hereof, Tenant shall surrender the Premises in broom clean condition, and in as good a state and condition as they were at the commencement of this Agreement, reasonable use and wear-and-tear thereof and damages by the elements excepted.

17. **ANIMALS.** Tenant shall be entitled to keep no more than _____ (___) domestic dogs, cats or birds; however, at such time as Tenant shall actually keep any such animal on the Premises, Tenant shall pay to Landlord a pet deposit of _____ DOLLARS ($_____), _____ DOLLARS ($_____) of which shall be non-refundable and shall be used upon the termination or expiration of this Agreement for the purposes of cleaning the carpets of the building.

18. **QUIET ENJOYMENT.** Tenant, upon payment of all of the sums referred to herein as being payable by Tenant and Tenant's performance of all Tenant's agreements contained herein and Tenant's observance of all rules and regulations, shall and may peacefully and quietly have, hold and enjoy said Premises for the term hereof.

19. **INDEMNIFICATION.** Landlord shall not be liable for any damage or injury of or to the Tenant, Tenant's family, guests, invitees, agents or employees or to any person entering the Premises or the building of which the Premises are a part or to goods or equipment, or in the structure or equipment of the structure of which the Premises are a part, and Tenant hereby agrees to indemnify, defend and hold Landlord harmless from any and all claims or assertions of every kind and nature.

20. **DEFAULT.** If Tenant fails to comply with any of the material provisions of this Agreement, other than the covenant to pay rent, or of any present rules and regulations or any that may be hereafter prescribed by Landlord, or materially fails to comply with any duties imposed on Tenant by statute, within seven (7) days after delivery of written notice by Landlord specifying the non-compliance and indicating the intention of Landlord to termi-

nate the Lease by reason thereof, Landlord may terminate this Agreement. If Tenant fails to pay rent when due and the default continues for seven (7) days thereafter, Landlord may, at Landlord's option, declare the entire balance of rent payable hereunder to be immediately due and payable and may exercise any and all rights and remedies available to Landlord at law or in equity or may immediately terminate this Agreement.

21.   **LATE CHARGE.**  In the event that any payment required to be paid by Tenant hereunder is not made within three (3) days of when due, Tenant shall pay to Landlord, in addition to such payment or other charges due hereunder, a "late fee" in the amount of _____DOLLARS ($_____).

22.   **ABANDONMENT.**  If at any time during the term of this Agreement Tenant abandons the Premises or any part thereof, Landlord may, at Landlord's option, obtain possession of the Premises in the manner provided by law, and without becoming liable to Tenant for damages or for any payment of any kind whatever. Landlord may, at Landlord's discretion, as agent for Tenant, relet the Premises, or any part thereof, for the whole or any part thereof, of the then unexpired term, and may receive and collect all rent payable by virtue of such reletting, and, at Landlord's option, hold Tenant liable for any difference between the rent that would have been payable under this Agreement during the balance of the unexpired term, if this Agreement had continued in force, and the net rent for such period realized by Landlord by means of such reletting. If Landlord's right of reentry is exercised following abandonment of the Premises by Tenant, then Landlord shall consider any personal property belonging to Tenant and left on the Premises to also have been abandoned, in which case Landlord may dispose of all such personal property in any manner Landlord shall deem proper and Landlord is hereby relieved of all liability for doing so.

23.   **ATTORNEYS' FEES.**  Should it become necessary for Landlord to employ an attorney to enforce any of the conditions or covenants hereof, including the collection of rentals or gaining possession of the Premises, Tenant agrees to pay all expenses so incurred, including a reasonable attorney's fee.

24.   **RECORDING OF AGREEMENT.**  Tenant shall not record this Agreement on the Public Records of any public office. In the event that Tenant shall record this Agreement, this Agreement shall, at Landlord's option, terminate immediately and Landlord shall be entitled to all rights and remedies that it has at law or in equity.

25.   **GOVERNING LAW.**  This Agreement shall be governed, construed and interpreted by, through and under the Laws of the State of Illinois.

26.   **SEVERABILITY.**  If any provision of this Agreement or the application thereof shall, for any reason and to any extent, be invalid or unenforceable, neither the remainder of this Agreement nor the application of the provision to other persons, entities or circumstances shall be affected thereby, but instead shall be enforced to the maximum extent permitted by law.

27.   **BINDING EFFECT.**  The covenants, obligations and conditions herein contained shall be binding on and inure to the benefit of the heirs, legal representatives, and assigns of the parties hereto.

28. **DESCRIPTIVE HEADINGS.** The descriptive headings used herein are for convenience of reference only and they are not intended to have any effect whatsoever in determining the rights or obligations of the Landlord or Tenant.

29. **CONSTRUCTION.** The pronouns used herein shall include, where appropriate, either gender or both, singular and plural.

30. **NON-WAIVER.** No indulgence, waiver, election or non-election by Landlord under this Agreement shall affect Tenant's duties and liabilities hereunder.

31. **MODIFICATION.** The parties hereby agree that this document contains the entire agreement between the parties and this Agreement shall not be modified, changed, altered or amended in any way except through a written amendment signed by all of the parties hereto.

32. **NOTICE.** Any notice required or permitted under this Lease or under state law shall be deemed sufficiently given or served if sent by United States certified mail, return receipt requested, addressed as follows:

If to Landlord to:

If to Tenant to:

Landlord and Tenant shall each have the right from time to time to change the place notice is to be given under this paragraph by written notice thereof to the other party. In addition, Landlord may provide notice to Tenant by posting notice upon the front door of the Premises.

33. **ADDITIONAL PROVISIONS; DISCLOSURES.**

_____
_____
_____
_____

[Landlord should note above any disclosures about the premises that may be required under Federal or State law, such as known lead-based paint hazards in the Premises. The Landlord should also disclose any flood hazards. Also any related agreements such as an "Option To Purchase" should be noted here.]

**As to Landlord this** _____ **day of** _____, 20_____.

LANDLORD

Sign: _____ Print: _____ Date: _____

**As to Tenant, this** _____ **day of** _____, 20_____.

TENANT(S)

Sign: _____ Print: _____ Date: _____

Sign: _____ Print: _____ Date: _____

# Option to Purchase Agreement

THIS AGREEMENT made and entered into on this _____ day of _____,
20_____ by and between _____
hereinafter called "Lessor", and _____
hereinafter called "Lessee."

The Lessor, for and in consideration of a non-refundable, option payment of $_____
dollars, paid by Lessee, receipt of which is hereby acknowledged, hereby grants Lessee an
option to purchase the property situated in the City of _____,
County of _____, State of _____, commonly known as:

Property Address: _____
Personal Property Included: _____
_____

The aforementioned option-payment is to be applied, 100%, to the purchase price of the
property provided Lessee exercises the option during the option period and actually closes
on the property within forty-five days of exercising said option. The aforementioned option
payment will NOT be refunded in the event Lessee fails to either exercise the option, or
fails to close on the property within forty-five days of exercising the option.

UPON THE FOLLOWING TERMS AND CONDITIONS:

1. ASSOCIATED LEASE: This option to purchase is associated with and made a part of
   the lease agreement entered into by and between the parties dated the _____
   day of _____, 20 _____. Any default, or breach on the part of Lessee
   with respect to said lease will void the terms of this option to purchase and will cause
   Lessee to forfeit all option payments and rent credits.

2. OPTION PERIOD: The term hereof commences on _____, 20 _____ and
   continues for an initial option period of _____ months thereafter, up to and
   including _____, 20 _____.
   a. Upon sixty-days written notice to the Lessor, and upon payment of an addi-
      tional, non-refundable, option payment of $ _____ dollars, Lessee may
      extend the term of this Option to Purchase Agreement an additional twelve
      months beyond the initial option period.

3. OPTION PRICE: Lessee may exercise this option at any time during the initial option
   period for a purchase price of $ _____, however:
   a. Should Lessee elect to extend the term of this agreement beyond the initial
      option period as per paragraph "2-a" of this agreement, the purchase price will
      increase to $ _____.
   b. Lessee is responsible for obtaining financing, and for all customary buyer closing
      costs, and fees including, but not limited to: lender costs and fees, inspections,
      surveys, title insurance, attorney fees, municipal fees, transfer taxes and stamps,
      etc.
   c. Lessee will forfeit all rights under this agreement if Lessee does not close on the
      property within forty-five days of exercising this option.

4.    RENT CREDIT TOWARD PURCHASE: _____% of monthly rent payments will be applied towards the purchase of the property provided that Lessee is not behind on any rental payments, or fees, at the time of exercising the option to purchase.

   a. Rent credits are non-refundable and non-transferable in the event Lessee fails to exercise the option, or fails to close on the property within forty-five days thereof.

   b. Rent credits do not accrue interest.

   c. Rent is due on the _____ day of every month during the term of this agreement. A rent credit toward purchase will only be given for rent payments received on or before 11:59 pm on the _____ day of the month. **Rent payments received after 11:59 pm on the _____ day of the month will NOT receive a rent credit towards purchase for that month.**

5.    MAINTENANCE, REPAIRS OR ALTERATIONS:  Lessee will maintain the premises in a clean and sanitary manner, including all equipment, appliances, fixtures, furniture and furnishings therein, and will surrender the same at the termination of the lease (if the option to purchase has not been exercised and/or the sale not closed) in as good a condition as received, normal wear-and-tear excepted.

   a. Lessee will be responsible for the full amount of damages caused by his/her negligence and that of his/her family, invitees, and guests.

   b. Lessee will maintain, at his/her own expense, any surrounding grounds, including lawns and shrubbery, and keep the same clear of rubbish and weeds, if such grounds are a part of the premises.

   c. Lessee will pay for all necessary repairs costing less than, and up to $_____ each month. Necessary repairs that are not due to the negligence of Lessee, and costing more than $ _____ will be paid by the Lessor.

   d. Lessee will make no alterations or additions to the structure, nor install, attach, connect, or maintain on the premises, or any part of the structure, interior or exterior, major appliances or devices of any kind without, in each and every case obtaining the written consent of Lessor and then, if granted, only upon the terms and conditions specified in such written consent.

   e. Lessee must obtain specific written permission, which will not be unreasonably withheld, for each and every pet or animal, and Lessee agrees to retain full responsibility for ALL damages associated with said pets and animals, irrespective of paragraph "5-c" of this agreement. Lessor will not pay for any pet/animal related damages, regardless of cost.

6.    ASSIGNMENT:  Lessee may not assign this agreement without the written consent of the Lessor, which will not be unreasonably withheld, provided that:

   a. The party to whom Lessee wishes to assign the premises to meets or exceeds Lessor's credit screening, background check, and pre-approval standards, and said assignee provides a completed and executed application form (to be provided by Lessor) to Lessor along with any requested application fee.

   b. Lessee remains secondarily liable for all rents, damages, and fees that may accrue subsequent to the assignment.

7.  DAMAGES:  In the event Lessee fails to exercise the option, or fails to close on the property within forty-five days of exercising the option, all option payments, rents, and repair costs paid will be forfeited as full liquidated damages.

8.  STATUS OF PAYMENTS:  Any and all up-front or subsequent option payments, rent credits, or repair costs are non-refundable; they do not accrue interest and they may not be applied to current rents, back rents, future rents, fees, repairs, or deposits.

9.  FURTHER AGREEMENTS:

    a. The headings or captions of paragraphs hereof are for identification purposes only and do not limit or construe the contents of the paragraphs.

    b. The invalidity, or unenforceability of any provision hereof will not affect or impact any other provision.

    c. Lessee agrees that Lessor may at any time and as often as desired assign or re-assign all of its rights as Lessor under this agreement.

    d. The obligations of two or more persons designated Lessee in this agreement will be joint and several.

    e. The recording of this option, or any memorandum thereof, will result in the automatic revocation of this option, and all monies paid to Landlord by tenant will be retained by Landlord as liquidated damages. In addition, Tenant will be liable to Landlord for all incidental and consequential damages for slander of title, including, but not limited to, attorney fees and court costs for correcting title.

10.  TIME IS OF THE ESSENCE IN ALL MATTERS OF THIS AGREEMENT.

11.  OTHER: _____
_____
_____

The undersigned agree to lease, with option to purchase, on the above terms, have read, fully understand and verify the above information as being correct. All parties acknowledge that this is a legally binding contract and are advised to seek the counsel of an attorney.

Lessor Name: _____

Signature: _____
                                                                     Date

Lessee Name: _____

Signature: _____
                                                                     Date

Lessee Name: _____

Signature: _____
                                                                     Date

## Resources

Here is a list of useful resources:

**MrLandlord.com**
http://www.mrlandlord.com

**Landlord.com**
http://www.landlord.com

**Tenant Verification Services, Inc.**
http://www.tenantverification.com

**The Complete Real Estate Software Catalog**
http://z-law.com

**American Demographics**
http://www.Demographics.com

**Bureau of Justice Statistics**
http://www.ojp.usdoj.gov/bjs

**Bureau of Labor Statistics**
http://www.bls.gov/home.htm

**Bureau of Transportation Statistics**
http://www.bts.gov

**U.S. Dept. of Commerce, U.S. Census Bureau**
http://www.census.gov

**FedStats**
http://www.fedstats.gov

**Gallup Organization**
http://www.gallup.com

**National Archives and Records Administration**
http://www.gpoaccess.gov/cfr/index.html

**National Center for Education Statistics**
http://nces.ed.gov

**National Center for Health Statistics**
http://www.cdc.gov/nchs

## Bibliography

Following are some of the books that have most influenced me with respect to economics, investing, political economy, wealth creation, and financial freedom. If you are serious about wealth creation and achieving financial freedom, I highly recommend that you read each and every one of these:

1. *How I Found Freedom in an Unfree World* (Harry Browne)

2. *What Has Government Done to Our Money* (Murray N. Rothbard)

3. *Human Action: A Treatise on Economics* (Ludwig von Mises)

4. *Economics in One Lesson* (Henry Hazlitt)

5. *Rich Dad, Poor Dad* (Robert T. Kiyosaki and Sharon L. Lechter)

6. *Rich Dad's Guide to Investing* (Robert T. Kiyosaki and Sharon L. Lechter)

7. *Cashflow Quadrant* (Robert T. Kiyosaki and Sharon L. Lechter)

8. *The Millionaire Real Estate Investor* (Gary Keller, Dave Jenks, and Jay Papasan)

9. The U.S. Constitution.

10. The U.S. Declaration of Independence.

11. *Confessions of An Economic Hit Man* (John Perkins)

12. *The E-Myth Revisited* (Michael E. Gerber).

## Real Estate Dictionary

**Abstract** – The notes made by a title examiner based on his examination of the land records. These notes are a concise summary of the transactions affecting the property. The title agency produces a *Binder* from the information in the abstract.

**Acceleration clause** – A condition in a real estate financing instrument giving the lender the power to declare all sums owing lender immediately due and payable upon the happening of an event, such as the sale of the property or a delinquency in the repayment of the note.

**Accretion** – The buildup of land from natural forces such as wind or water.

**Acknowledgement** – As a verb, the confirmation by a party executing a legal document that this is his signature and voluntary act. This confirmation is made to an authorized officer of the Court or notary public who signs a statement also called an acknowledgment.

**Acre** – 43,560 square feet of land.

**Addendum** – A form/document added to a contract or agreement also known as a Rider.

**Adjustable rate mortgage (arm)** – A mortgage loan which bears interest at a rate subject to change during the term of the loan.

**Adjustment interval** – On an adjustable rate mortgage, the time between changes in the interest rate and/or monthly payment, typically one, three or five years, depending on the index.

**Administrator** – A person appointed by the Court to settle the estate of a person who dies without a will. The feminine form is Administratrix. Compare, EXECUTOR.

**Adverse possession** – A claim made against land titled to another person based on open, notorious and hostile possession and use of the land to the exclusion of the titled owner.

**Agency** – A relationship in which the agent is given the authority to act on behalf of another person, the Principal.

**Agreement** – A meeting of minds.

**Air rights** – The right to the air space above real property.

**ALTA owner's policy** – A type of title insurance policy issued by title insurance companies, which expands the risks normally insured against under the standard type of policy to include unrecorded mechanic's liens, unrecorded physical easements, facts that a physical survey would show, water and mineral rights; and rights of parties in possession, such as tenants' and buyers' rights under unrecorded instruments.

**Amendment** – A change to the correct document or alteration to the original document/agreement without changing its principal essence.

**Amortization** – The periodic principal pay down of a loan.

**Amortized Loan** – A loan to be repaid, interest and principal, by a series of regular payments that are equal or nearly equal, without any special balloon payment prior to maturity.

**Annual Percentage Rate (APR)** – An interest rate reflecting the cost of a mortgage as a yearly rate. This rate is likely to be higher than the stated note rate or advertised rate on the mortgage because it takes into account points and other credit costs. The APR allows home buyers to compare different types of mortgages based on the annual cost for each loan.

**Appraisal** – An estimate of the value of property made by a qualified professional called an appraiser. Most states require licenses. Various lenders have their own lists of approved appraisers.

**Appurtenance** – Anything attached to the land (or used with it) that passes to the new owner.

**Assessment** – A local tax levied against a property for a specific purpose, such as a sewer or streetlights.

**Assign** – To transfer interest.

**Assignee** – One who receives an assignment or transfer of rights. An assignment of a contract transfers the right to buy property.

**Assignor** – The one who assigns to another person.

**Assumption** – The agreement between buyer and seller where the buyer takes over the payments on an existing mortgage from the seller. Assuming a loan usually saves the buyer money since this is an existing mortgage debt, unlike a new mortgage where closing costs and new, possibly higher, market-rate interest charges will apply.

**Attachment** – Seizure of property through Court process to repay a debt.

**Attorney in Fact** – A type of agency relationship where one person holds a *Power of Attorney* allowing him to execute legal documents on behalf of another. Decisions made by the *Attorney in Fact* are binding on the principal.

**Balloon** – Usually a short-term fixed-rate loan involving small payments for a certain period of time and one large payment for the remainder of the principal at a time specified by contract.

**Bankruptcy** – A provision of Federal Law whereby a debtor surrenders his assets to the Bankruptcy Court and is relieved of the future obligation to repay his unsecured debts. A Trustee in Bankruptcy administers the assets, selling them to pay as much of the debt as possible. If your seller is in bankruptcy, the Trustee in Bankruptcy owns the property and is the party who signs the contract and makes decisions. After bankruptcy, the debtor is discharged and his unsecured creditors may not pursue further collection efforts against him. Secured creditors, those holding deeds of trust or judgment liens, continue to be secured by the property but they may not take other action to collect from the debtor.

**Benchmark** – A permanent reference mark for surveyors.

**Beneficiary** – A person named to receive a benefit from a TRUST.

**Bid** – An offer.

**Binder** – A title insurance binder is the written commitment of a title insurance company to insure title to the property subject to its specified conditions and exclusions.

**Blanket Mortgage** – A mortgage covering at least two pieces of real estate as security for the same mortgage. This sort of loan is more common for commercial property or "special case" loans.

**Bond** – An amount of money, often posted with the Court, to guarantee against loss as a result of a possible claim. For example, if there is a LIEN against the property, the owner may post a bond to remove the lien and the parties argue over the money rather than the property.

**Breach of Contract** – Failure to perform provisions of a contract.

**Broker** – A middleman responsible for brining buyers and sellers/users and providers together, in exchange for a fee. May assist with negotiations between the parties.

**Building Codes** – Local building laws to promote safe practices in the design and construction of buildings.

**Buyer's Market** – A situation where there is an overabundance of supply relative to interested buyers.

**By-laws** – Rules and regulations governing an association or corporation.

**Capital Gains** – Profit earned from a sale of real estate.

**Capitalization** – A method used to estimate value of a property based on the rate of return on investment.

**Cash Flow** – The amount of cash derived over a certain period of time from an income-producing property. The cash flow should be large enough to pay the expenses of the income-producing property.

**Caveat Emptor** – "Let the buyer beware." The idea that a buyer must inspect a property and be satisfied that it is adequate for his needs, with the seller having no obligation to disclose defects. Mostly applies, if at all, to commercial property sales; many states have enacted mandatory seller disclosure laws with respect to the sale of residential property

**CC&R's** – Covenants, conditions, and restrictions. The basic rules establishing the rights and obligations of owners of real property within a subdivision or other tract of land in relation to other owners within the same subdivision or tract and in relation to an association of owners organized for the purpose of operating and maintaining property commonly owned by the individual owners.

**Certificate of Eligibility** – The document given to qualified veterans entitling them to VA guaranteed loans for homes, business, and mobile homes. Certificates of eligibility may be obtained by sending DD-214 (Separation Paper) to the local VA office with VA form 1880 (request for Certificate of Eligibility).

**Certificate of Occupancy** – A certificate issued by a local governmental body stating that the building is in a condition to be occupied.

**Certificate of Satisfaction** – A document signed by the Noteholder and recorded in the land records evidencing release of a *Deed Of Trust, Mortgage* or other lien on the property.

**Certificate of Title** – A written opinion by an attorney setting forth the status of title to the property as shown on the public records. The certificate does not certify as to matters not of record and affords no protection unless the author was negligent. See *Title Insurance.*

**Chain of Title** – The series of transactions from *Grantor* to *Grantee* as evidenced in the land records.

**Chattel** – Personal property.

**Class Action** – A claim brought up on behalf of a group of people.

**Closing** – The meeting between the buyer, seller and lender or their agents where the property and funds legally change hands. Also called settlement. Closing costs usually include an origination fee, discount points, appraisal fee, title search and insurance, survey, taxes, deed recording fee, credit report and notary fees.

**Cloud on Title** – An evidence of encumbrances.

**Coinsurance** – When more than one insurance company shares the risk of a particular transaction or series of transactions. Lenders may require co-insurance on large commercial projects.

**Collateral** – Property pledged to secure a loan.

**Condemnation** – The governmental taking of private property for a public use through the exercise of the power of *Eminent Domain.* By law, the owner must receive fair compensation for their property.

**Condominium** – A system of individual *Fee Simple* ownership of units in a multi-unit structure, combined with joint ownership of common areas. Each individual may sell or encumber his own unit.

**Conservator** – Also called *Guardian*, a person designated by the Court to protect and preserve the property of someone who is not able to manage his/her own affairs. Examples include the mentally incompetent, minors and incarcerated persons.

**Construction Loan** – A short-term interim loan to pay for the construction of buildings or homes. Usually paid out periodically as the construction progresses, with the lender approving each stage of the construction prior to releasing additional funds.

**Contract** – A lawful agreement between parties, usually in writing, and enforceable in a court of law.

**Contract for Deed** – Also known as a *Land Contract* or *Installment Contract*. A method of financing where title remains in the Seller's name until the Buyer has paid the full purchase price.

**Conventional Loan** – A mortgage not insured by FHA or guaranteed by the VA.

**Cooperative (Co-op)** – A system of individual ownership of stock in a corporation that, in turn, owns the structure. Each owner has an exclusive right to use his individual unit and must pay his portion of the debt encumbering the entire building.

**Cost Approach** – A method used by appraisers to estimate the value of a property, which is based on the costs of materials.

**Co-tenancy** – General term used to describe real property owned by more than one party. For specific forms of co-tenancy see: *Tenants In Common, Joint Tenants, Tenants By The Entirety*.

**Covenant** – A written agreement or restriction on the use of land, or the promise of certain acts. Homeowner Associations often enforce restrictive covenants governing architectural controls and maintenance responsibilities. However, land could be subject to restrictive covenants even if there is no homeowner's association.

**Credit Report** – A report documenting the credit history and current status of a borrower's credit standing.

**Debt-to-income Ratio** – The ratio, expressed as a percentage, which results when a borrower's monthly payment obligation on long-term debts is divided by his or her gross monthly income. See housing expenses-to-income ratio.

**Deed** – The written document conveying real property.

**Deed of Trust** – A voluntary lien to secure a debt deeding the property to Trustees who foreclose or sell the property at public auction, in the event of default on the Note that the Deed of Trust secures.

**Default** – Failure to meet legal obligations in a contract. Specifically, failure to make the monthly payments on a mortgage.

**Deferred Interest** – When a mortgage is written with a monthly payment that is less than required to satisfy the note rate, the unpaid interest is deferred by adding it to the loan balance. See *Negative Amortization.*

**Deficiency Judgment** – If a foreclosure sale does not bring sufficient proceeds to pay the costs of sale and the note in full, the holder of the note may obtain a judgment against the foreclosed upon party.

**Delivery** – The final, unconditional and absolute transfer of a *Deed* to the Grantee so that the Grantor may not revoke it. A signed Deed that is held by the Grantor does not pass title.

**Dower** – A spouse's interest in the property of a deceased spouse.

**Down Payment** – Money paid to make up the difference between the purchase price and the mortgage amount.

**Due On Sale Clause** – A provision in a mortgage enabling the lender to demand full repayment if the borrower sells the mortgaged property.

**Earnest Money** – A good faith deposit that accompanies an offer to purchase.

**Easement** – The right (temporary or permanent) to use the land of another for a specific limited purpose. Examples include utility lines, driveways, and *Ingress* and *Egress*.

**Eminent Domain** – The government's power to take private property for public use upon payment of just compensation.

**Encroachment** – The physical intrusion of a structure or improvement on the land of another. An example would be a fence over a property line.

**Encumbrance** – Any lien, liability or charge against a property.

**Equal Credit Opportunity Act** – A federal law that requires lenders and other creditors to make credit equally available without discrimination based on race, color, religion, national origin, age, sex, marital status or receipt of income from public assistance programs.

**Equity** – The difference between the fair market value and current indebtedness; also referred to as the owner's interest. The value in real estate held by the owner over and above the obligation against the property.

**Equity Sharing** – A form of joint ownership between an owner/occupant and an owner/investor. The investor takes depreciation deductions for his share of the ownership. The occupant receives a portion of the tax write-offs for interest and taxes and a part of his monthly payment is treated as rent. The co-owners divide the profit upon sale of the property. See *Joint Ownership Agreement*.

**Escheat** – Property that reverts to the state when an individual dies without heirs and without a will.

**Escrow** – A disinterested third party holds funds or documents on behalf of others and subject to their instructions.

**Executor** – A person named in a will to carry out its terms and administer the estate. The feminine form is Executrix. See *Administrator*.

**Federal Home Loan Mortgage Corporation (FHLMC)**
– Affiliate of the Federal Home Loan Bank, which creates a secondary money market in conventional residential loans and in FHA and VA loans by purchasing mortgage loans from members of the Federal Reserve System and the Federal Home Loan Bank Systems.

**Fee Simple** – The absolute total interest in real property.

**Fiduciary Relationship** – A relationship of trust and confidence between a principal and agent (or lawyer and client, or doctor and patient, etc.).

**Fixture** – An item of personal property attached to real property so that it cannot be removed without damage to the real property. A fixture becomes part of the real property.

**Foreclosure** – The process by which a lender sells property securing a loan in order to repay the loan. Under a *Deed Of Trust*, foreclosure is by public auction after appropriate advertisement. A *Mortgage* may require the lender to obtain Court approval prior to sale.

**General Warranty Deed** – The Grantor warrants title against all claims. Deed type with the most warranties.

**Graduated Payment Mortgage (GPM)** – A type of flexible-payment mortgage where the payments increase for a specified period of time and then level off.

**Grantee** – The person receiving an interest in property.

**Grantor** – The person granting, selling or giving up an interest in property.

**Gross Income** – Income before expenses.

**Ground Lease** – The owner grants a long-term lease of the land (usually 99 years) and allows the lessee to build and use the land as agreed. At the end of the term, the land and all improvements revert to the owner.

**Hazard Insurance** – A form of insurance in which the insurance company protects the insured from specified losses such as fire, windstorm and the like.

**Housing Ratio** – The ratio, expressed as a percentage, which results when a borrower's housing expenses are divided by his/her gross monthly income. See *Debt-to-income Ratio.*

**Impound** – That portion of a borrower's monthly payments held by the lender or servicer to pay for taxes, hazard insurance, mortgage insurance, lease payments, and other items as they become due. Also known as reserves.

**Income Approach** – An appraisal approach that uses a property's income to estimate value.

**Indemnity** – A protection against actual loss or damage as a result of the matter mentioned. An indemnity is not an absolute guarantee that something won't happen; it states the terms under which an actual loss will be compensated.

**Index** – A published interest rate against which lenders measure the difference between the current interest rate on an adjustable rate mortgage and that earned by other investments (such as one-, three-, and five-year U.S. Treasury security yields, or the consumer price index), which is then used to adjust the interest rate on an adjustable mortgage.

**Ingress and Egress** – Applied to EASEMENTS, meaning the right to go in and out over a piece of property but not the right to park on it.

**Initial Note Rate** – With regard to an adjustable rate mortgage, the note rate upon origination. This rate may differ from and is usually less than the fully indexed rate.

**Insurable Title** – Title subject to a defect or claim, which a title insurance company is willing to insure against. See *Marketable Title*.

**Interim Financing** – A construction loan made during completion of a building or a project. A permanent loan usually replaces this loan after completion.

**Joint Ownership Agreement** – An agreement between owners defining their rights, ownership, monetary obligations and responsibilities. This could be between and investor and an occupant or the occupants. If an investor is involved, the investor does not take depreciation deductions and none of the occupant's payment is deemed rent for tax purposes. See *Equity Sharing*.

**Joint Tenancy** – Two or more persons owning a property with the right of survivorship, meaning that the survivor inherits the property without reference to the decedent's will. Creditors may sue to have the property divided to settle claims against one of the owners.

**Judgment Lien** – A judgment is a lien against real property that is imposed by a judge.

**Jumbo Loan** – A loan that is larger than the limits set by the Federal National Mortgage Association and the Federal Home Loan Mortgage Corporation. Because jumbo loans cannot be funded by these two agencies, they usually carry a higher interest rate.

**Junior Mortgage** – Mortgage of lesser priority than the prior recorded mortgage.

**Land Contract** – See *Contract For Deed*.

**Leasehold Estate** – Tenant's right of possession for a specific period of time under a lease agreement.

**Lease Option** – A rental agreement that includes the right, but not the obligation, to purchase the rented property for a specified price, on or before some future specified date. Usually includes rent credits if the option is exercised and the property is purchased.

**Lifetime Cap** – With regard to an adjustable rate mortgage, a ceiling that the note rate cannot exceed over the life of the loan.

**Life Estate** – The right to use, occupy and own for the life of an individual. See *Fee Simple*.

**Lis Pendens** – Recorded document showing a pending litigation filed in the court. These show up on the preliminary title report and must be dealt with when transferring ownership or refinancing.

**Loan Application** – The source of information on which the lender bases its decision to make the loan; defines the term of the loan, gives the name(s) of the borrower(s), place of employment, salary, bank accounts and credit references, and describes the real estate that is to be mortgaged. It also stipulates the amount of the loan being applied for and the repayment terms.

**Loan-to-value Ratio (LTV)** – The relationship between the amount of the mortgage loan and the value of the property expressed as a percentage.

**Majority** – The age at which a person may handle his own affairs.

**Margin** – The amount a lender adds to the index on an adjustable rate mortgage to establish the adjusted interest rate.

**Market Value** – A range of value that describes what a property would likely sell for in an open market transaction.

**Marketable Title** – A title without defects or claims. See *Insurable Title*.

**Mechanic's Lien** – The right of an unpaid contractor, laborer or supplier to file a lien against property to recover the value of his work.

**Metes and Bounds** – A means of legally describing land that indicates its boundaries by giving directions and distances from some beginning point.

**Mortgage** – The pledge of real property as security for a debt. To foreclose, the lender must often institute a court action and the borrower may have the right to reclaim the property via a right of redemption.

**Mortgage Insurance Premium (MIP)** – Money paid to insure the mortgage when the down payment is less than 20 percent. See private mortgage insurance, FHA mortgage insurance.

**Mortgagee** – A lender that accepts the pledge of real property as collateral for a loan.

**Mortgagor** – A borrower that pledges real property as collateral for a loan.

**Negative Amortization** – Occurs when monthly payments are not large enough to pay all of the interest due on a loan. Unpaid interest is added to the unpaid balance of the loan.

**Net Worth** – The difference between total assets and total liabilities.

**Non-assumption Clause** – A statement in a mortgage contract forbidding the assumption of the mortgage without prior approval of the lender.

**Non-performing Loan** – A loan in default. A loan where no payments are being made.

**Notary Public** – One authorized by law to acknowledge and certify documents and signatures.

**Note** – A written promise to pay a certain sum of money at a certain time.

**Offer** – A proposal. After acceptance, it becomes a contract.

**Option** – A right given for a consideration to keep an offer to purchase or lease open for a specific time.

**Partition** – The forced division of land among parties who were formerly co-owners. A partition suit may seek to divide the land or, if not practical, sell the land and divide the proceeds.

**Pay-off Amount** – A total balance; the amount of a full payment on an existing loan or lien.

**PITI** – Principal, Interest, Taxes, and Insurance. This total is called the monthly housing expense.

**Plat** – A map showing the division of a piece of land with lots, streets and, if applicable, common area.

**PMI** – See *Private Mortgage Insurance.*

**Points** – Prepaid interest assessed by the lender at closing. Each point is equal to 1% of the loan amount (e.g., two points on a $100,000 mortgage would cost $2,000).

**Power of Attorney** – A written document authorizing another to act on his behalf as an *Attorney In Fact.* One does not need to be a licensed attorney to act as an attorney in fact, but power of attorney forms are powerful legal documents that should be used only under advice of a licensed attorney at law.

**Prepayment Penalty** – An additional charge imposed by the lender for paying off a loan before the due date.

**Prime Rate** – The most favorable interest rate charged by lenders on short-term loans to qualified customers.

**Private Mortgage Insurance (PMI)** – In the event that you do not have a 20 percent down payment, lenders may allow a smaller down payment. With the smaller down payment loans, however, borrowers are usually required to carry private mortgage insurance. Private mortgage insurance usually requires an initial premium payment and may require an additional monthly fee depending on your loan structure.

**Probate** – Court process to prove a valid will.

**Promissory Note** – A written unsecured note promising to pay a specified amount of money on demand, transferable to a third party.

**Public Sale** – Sale or auction open to the public.

**Purchase Money Mortgage** – Seller financing as a part of the purchase price.

**Quiet Title Suit** – A suit brought to remove a claim or objection on title.

**Quitclaim Deed** – A deed releasing whatever interest you may hold in a property but making no warranty whatsoever. See *Special Warranty Deed* and *General Warranty Deed*.

**Realtor®** – A member of the National Association of Realtors.

**Recision** – The cancellation of a contract.

**Recording Fees** – Money paid to the lender for recording a home sale with the local authorities, thereby making it part of the public records.

**Refinance** – Obtaining a new mortgage loan on a property already owned, often to replace existing loans on the property.

**Reissue Rate** – A discounted rate for title insurance when the title was previously insured with an owner's title insurance policy issued within the last ten years.

**Remainder** – An interest in land that is postponed until the termination of some other interest such as a LIFE ESTATE.

**Rent to Own** – See *Lease Option*.

**Reversion** – A provision in a conveyance that the land will return to the grantor upon the happening of an event or contingency.

**Riparian Rights** – The rights of an owner of land to water in adjacent rivers and/or streams.

**Second Mortgage** – A mortgage recorded after a First mortgage, ranking second in priority.

**Secondary Market** – A market whose purpose is the purchase and sale of existing mortgages, usually at discounted prices, to provide greater liquidity to the mortgagee/lender.

**Seller's Market** – A situation where there is an overabundance of demand relative to supply.

**Special Warranty Deed** – The seller guarantees he has done nothing to impair the title but makes no warranty prior to his ownership. See *General Warranty Deed* and *Quitclaim Deed*.

**Specific Performance** – A legal action to complete the performance of a contract.

**Statute of Limitations** – The time period allowed to file a lawsuit to enforce a claim, after which time it is barred by law.

**Subdivision** – Dividing land into lots and streets. The owner signs a PLAT and Deed of Resubdivision, which is recorded among the land records. The state and county may have strict requirements for the subdivision of land.

**Tenants By The Entirety** – A form of co-ownership between a husband and wife. The husband and wife have a right of survivorship in the property, and neither may sue the other to *partition* the property. A creditor of only one of them may not claim the property or the proceeds of sale.

**Tenants in Common** – Two or more persons own the property with no right of survivorship. If one dies, his interest passes to his heirs, not necessarily the co-owner. Either party, or a creditor of one, may sue to *partition* the property.

**Testate** – To die with a Will. See *Intestate.*

**Testator** – One who makes out a last will and testament. The feminine form is *Testatrix.*

**Title** – A document that gives evidence of an individual's ownership of property.

**Title Insurance** – Insurance that provides an *indemnity* against loss or damage as a result of defect in title ownership to a particular piece of property. Title insurance covers mistakes made during a *Title Search* as well as matters that could not be found or discovered in the public records such as missing heirs, mistakes, fraud and forgery. See *Certificate of Title.*

**Title Search** – An examination of the public records, including court decisions, to disclose facts concerning the ownership of real estate. The title examiner prepares an *abstract* and the title agent prepares a *binder.*

**Trust** – A right to or in property held for the benefit of another. A trust may be written or implied. An implied trust is called a Constructive Trust.

**Trustee** – One who holds property in Trust for another.

**Trustor** – One who gifts funds or assets to others by transferring fiduciary duty to a third party trustee that will maintain the assets for the benefit of the beneficiaries. Person who establishes a Trust.

**Two-step Mortgage** – A mortgage in which the borrower receives a below-market interest rate for a specified number of years (most often five or seven), and then receives a new interest rate adjusted (within certain limits) to market conditions at that time. The lender sometimes has the option to call the loan due with 30 days' notice at the end of five or seven years.

**Underwriting** – The decision about whether to make a loan to a potential borrower based on factors such as credit, employment, and assets, and the matching of this risk to an appropriate rate and term or loan amount.

**Usury** – Charging more than the maximum rate of interest that is legally permitted.

**VA Loan** – A loan guaranteed by the Department of Veterans Affairs. Restricted to individuals qualified by military service or other entitlements.

**Variable Rate Mortgage** – An adjustable rate mortgage.

**Verification of deposit** – A document signed by the borrower's financial institution verifying the status and balance of his/her financial accounts.

**Verification of Employment** – A document signed by the borrower's employer verifying his/her position and salary.

**Waiver** – Relinquishment of a right.

**Warranty Deed** – A deed conveying the title to a property with a warranty of clean, clear marketable title.

**Zoning** – Regulation by local government of use and development of private land.

## Available Supplementary Materials

✦ **Forms and Checklists on CD Plus FREE Bonus Materials** – all the forms and checklists from the book in Microsoft Word and PDF formats – modify forms and checklists to suit your needs, and save and print as needed. Also, an Excel Spreadsheet for deal analysis, proven ads that magnetically attract tenant/buyers, and a tested telephone script for your incoming ad calls.

**FREE Bonus #1:** Audio CD in which you'll hear the finer points of the *WealthLoop*™ philosophy explained. I've received enthusiastic comments from listeners who found this to be very helpful in clarifying certain aspects of the book, and many have found it to be the motivating *push* they needed to get themselves started—great for listening to in your car while you're riding through neighborhoods checking out properties. (A $14.97 value – FREE)

**FREE Bonus #2:** a complimentary copy of the quarterly "*Wealth-Loop*™ *Financial Freedom Newsletter.*" This context rich newsletter typically features explanations of advanced investing techniques, investing tips and advice, a question and answer section, interesting quotes and interviews, as well as a section on real world investing stories "from the trenches." (A $9.97 value – FREE)

**You get:** Forms CD, Excel Spreadsheet, Proven Ads, Tested Phone Script, Audio Interview CD, and Complimentary Newsletter, only **$19.97+FREE Shipping**

✦ **Real Estate Agent's Investor Business System** – take the proven principles of "Building Wealth Buying Houses" and create a business that can multiply your production almost instantly and with minimum effort.

- Build a "No Competition Zone" around your business.
- Create multiple, regular, *dependable income* streams.
- Generate **2–6 transactions per client**, per year.
- Become the *respected expert* that clients rely on.
- Gain **time freedom** and personal autonomy.

**You get:** ½-hr. Telephone Coaching Session, (7) step-by-step systems workbooks, ad templates, business planning tools, forms database, website template, telephone scripts, client qualification checklists, audio CD, and more . . .
(Details at www.WealthLoop.com). **$99.97+FREE Shipping**

## Quick Order Form

✆ **Fax orders:** 773-696-2109. Send this form.

▢ **Website Orders:** www.WealthLoop.com

✉ **Postal Orders:**  Brain Forge Press
Attn: WealthLoop Order
2106 N Clark
Chicago, IL 60614

**Please send the following books, disks, or reports.** I understand that I may return any of the following unopened items in saleable condition for a FULL REFUND for any reason, no questions asked.

| Item | Qty. | Unit $ | Total $ |
|---|---|---|---|
| Forms and Checklists CD (Plus FREE Bonuses) | _____ | $19.97 | $ _____ |
| Real Estate Agent's Investor Business System | _____ | $99.97 | $ _____ |
| Quarterly *"Financial Freedom"* Newsletter (1 yr) | _____ | $39.97 | $ _____ |
| Sub-Total ..................................................... | | | $ _____ |
| Sales Tax ...................................................... (Illinois residents please add 9.0%) | | | $ _____ |
| Total ............................................................ | | | $ _____ |

CC Type _____ CC# _____ Exp. Date: _____

(Visa, Master Card, AMEX, Discover, eCHECK, PayPal)

Name: _____

Address: _____

City: _____ State: _____ Zip: _____

Telephone: _____

Email Address: _____

### Please send more FREE information on:

❏ Agent Success Coaching     ❏ Investor Success Coaching

❏ Other Books                ❏ Courses/Seminars

❏ Speaking Events

# Quick Order Form

✆ **Fax orders:** 773-696-2109. Send this form.

🖥 **Website Orders:** www.WealthLoop.com

✉ **Postal Orders:**    Brain Forge Press
                      Attn: WealthLoop Order
                      2106 N Clark
                      Chicago, IL 60614

**Please send the following books, disks, or reports.** I understand that I may return any of the following unopened items in saleable condition for a FULL REFUND for any reason, no questions asked.

| Item | Qty. | Unit $ | Total $ |
|------|------|--------|---------|
| Forms and Checklists CD (Plus FREE Bonuses) | _____ | $19.97 | $ _____ |
| Real Estate Agent's Investor Business System | _____ | $99.97 | $ _____ |
| Quarterly *"Financial Freedom"* Newsletter (1 yr) | _____ | $39.97 | $ _____ |
| Sub-Total ....................................................... | | | $ _____ |
| Sales Tax ....................................................... (Illinois residents please add 9.0%) | | | $ _____ |
| Total ............................................................. | | | $ _____ |

CC Type _____ CC# _____ Exp. Date: _____
(Visa, Master Card, AMEX, Discover, eCHECK, PayPal)

Name: _____

Address: _____

City: _____ State: _____ Zip: _____

Telephone: _____

Email Address: _____

**Please send more FREE information on:**

❏ Agent Success Coaching    ❏ Investor Success Coaching

❏ Other Books    ❏ Courses/Seminars

❏ Speaking Events

## Quick Order Form

✆ **Fax orders:** 773-696-2109. Send this form.

💻 **Website Orders:** www.WealthLoop.com

✉ **Postal Orders:**   Brain Forge Press
Attn: WealthLoop Order
2106 N Clark
Chicago, IL 60614

**Please send the following books, disks, or reports.** I understand that I may return any of the following unopened items in saleable condition for a FULL REFUND for any reason, no questions asked.

| Item | Qty. | Unit $ | Total $ |
|---|---|---|---|
| Forms and Checklists CD (Plus FREE Bonuses) | _____ | $19.97 | $ _____ |
| Real Estate Agent's Investor Business System | _____ | $99.97 | $ _____ |
| Quarterly *"Financial Freedom"* Newsletter (1 yr) | _____ | $39.97 | $ _____ |
| Sub-Total ................................................... | | | $ _____ |
| Sales Tax ................................................... (Illinois residents please add 9.0%) | | | $ _____ |
| Total .......................................................... | | | $ _____ |

CC Type _____ CC# _____ Exp. Date: _____

(Visa, Master Card, AMEX, Discover, eCHECK, PayPal)

Name: _____

Address: _____

City: _____ State: _____ Zip: _____

Telephone: _____

Email Address: _____

**Please send more FREE information on:**

❏ Agent Success Coaching      ❏ Investor Success Coaching

❏ Other Books      ❏ Courses/Seminars

❏ Speaking Events

# Notes

# Notes

# Notes

# <u>Notes</u>

# Notes

# Notes

# Notes

# Notes